THE CAMPING SOURCEBOOK

··

Also by Steven A. Griffin

The
CAMPING
SOURCEBOOK

· ·

YOUR ONE-STOP RESOURCE FOR EVERYTHING YOU NEED FOR GREAT CAMPING

by

Steven A. Griffin

The
Globe
Pequot
Press

Old Saybrook, Connecticut

UPM 16.95

For Mary Jo
My beloved camping partner,
who has shared tents cold and warm, days festive and frustrating,
and meals fine and foul—and who through it all
has greeted each camping day
with a smile, a chuckle, and a hug for the author.

All photos are by the author unless otherwise credited
Illustrations by Maryann Dubé
Cover photo by Julie Bidwell. Equipment used in front cover photo courtesy of North Cove Outfitters, 75 Main Street, Old Saybrook, Connecticut, 06475; (860) 388–6585.

Library of Congress Cataloging-in-Publication Data
Griffin, Steven A.
    The camping sourcebook: your one-stop resource for everything you need for great camping / by Steven A. Griffin.
        p. cm.
    Includes bibliographical references (p.).
    ISBN: 0-7627-0042-4
    1. Camping—Handbooks, manuals, etc.   I. Title
    GV191.7.G76 1997
    796.54—dc21
                                                                        96-24.055
                                                                             CIP

Manufactured in the United States of America
First Edition/First Printing

Contents

Acknowledgments

Many people have been generous with their time, talents, and knowledge as this book was created. John Johnson, a seasoned backpacker, provided insight in several sections, and his assistance was particularly appreciated.

Some material in this book first appeared in slightly different form in other publications. We thank the editors of *Falcon* magazine, *Michigan Boating Annual*, *Country America*, *Outdoor Action*, and the *Midland* (Michigan) *Daily News* for permission to use material first seen in their publications.

These people and others have provided much of what's helpful here. Any errors must be laid to the author.

Introduction

Camping is a tradition; not a one-time event. We camp because of the fun on family, scout, or friends' outings. We want to recapture that joy, perhaps share it with kids of our own, and branch out in new camping directions. Even if we come to camping as adults, we quickly build a mental scrapbook of places, people, and events we enjoy while camping, and we are eager to add more pages to that book.

Making Memories

Creating that next camping memory is very much what this book is about. Camping seems a seesaw: simplicity on side; equipment on the other. The best camping trip, the most satisfying outing, is where we have with us every piece of equipment, every bite of food, we need. And nothing more. A standard bit of camping wisdom advises dividing gear upon return into three piles: things used frequently; things used a little; and things used not at all. List them, then take on your next trip only those things in the first pile that were used frequently. Except for safety and first aid items that should always be taken and hopefully never used, that remains great advice.

Elegance

Every camper and every camping trip is different, though, so no two lists of necessary items will be the same. The list will change over time and circumstance. New items call for testing, too.

We seek an *elegant* camp. The dictionary defines elegance as being luxurious, but in a refined, restrained manner. Classy. Simple and efficient. We want the well-appointed camp.

Pitching that camp—whether in the backcountry or in a modern resort campground—has never been easier. More well-designed equipment is available now than ever before.

The Camping Sourcebook is written to be a tour through a modern camping equipment store. Not every manufacturer is covered here, nor is every item. This is a taste of the variety, a hint of the choices available. I've included little of what is often called "technical" equipment, the super stuff you need if you'll be climbing mountains, spending weeks in the backcountry, and doing similar feats. I've included suggested retail prices when they were provided. I've used some of the manufacturer's own words in describing products. E-mail and website addresses of those firms and agencies that offered them are added, too.

There are sidebar discussions, sometimes playful and sometimes instructive, presented as journal entries. Several of them from journals I've kept on camping trips. Meander through the offerings, read a journal entry or two, and find a thing or two you'd like to try. Then pack up, and go camping.

Legal Stuff

Do you want to read a book whose most common letters are ®, ©, or ™? Neither do I. Brand names, trademarks, and copyrights are valuable property of the people who own them, and can't be treated lightly. Names that are capitalized in *The*

Camping Sourcebook are almost certainly registered brand or trade names. Only their owners can use them to designate an item. They're valuable intellectual property. Treat them as such!

Camping is a sport of infinite variety, pursued by all kinds of people, in all kinds of settings, with all kinds of equipment. This book focuses on vacation-style camping: weekend, week-in-the-summer, medium-tough backbacking, RV camping, even with some extreme camping thrown in.

Camping Stats

In one recent year alone, 55 million people camped in tents or in recreational vehicles. Even more people—64 million, according to a national survey—consider themselves campers. If we didn't get a chance to go this year, you can bet we have plans for next. The most recent U.S. Census Bureau Statistical Abstract of the United States cites camping as the fourth most popular participatory sport or activity in the nation.

When we camp, we generally have fewer things around us than we would at home. We're off somewhere on our own, so we count more heavily upon each item of that equipment. Quality well-chosen gear lasts longer. Gear that fails in the middle of a rainy night a long way from home is less economy than catastrophe. Good gear makes us "happy campers!"

Happy Campers

Any adult who isn't just a little bit afraid about taking one or more kids on a camping trip just doesn't understand the situation.

In the campground you hear everybody else's noises; they hear yours. There's no television, and too many mosquitoes, and it's too far to the bathroom in the middle of the night and, besides, the bathroom smells funny. The man in the next tent snores. His kids got to bring their electronic games, and you didn't let your kids bring theirs. All you big people want to do is snooze and read, and that's boring. Hey, look at this neat snake . . . .

Each year millions of us gather up the family, jam the sport utility full of cookware, sleepwear and shelter, to head out in search of outdoor adventure. We usually find it, too, although it's not always the experience we expect. But then, that's part of the fun.

Camping should mean adventure, something unexpected, some way in which we exceed our self-expectations. It needs to maintain a comfort level, too, a feeling in the gut that things are going to turn out all right.

When camping with kids, you have to cover those bases, but for the kid, not for you. There's no minimum age for camping. Infants, toddlers, pre-schoolers, and even teenagers make good camping companions, provided the experience matches their tastes and abilities.

You may like to backpack on wilderness trails along mountain ridges. Your kid may get the same thrill from walking the riverbank just outside town, 50 yards from a cabin tent pitched by your station wagon.

Marinated steaks grilled medium-rare over coals and served with asparagus and wine may be your perfect camp meal. It's likely that beanie-weenies washed down by hot chocolate and followed by s'mores will appeal to the junior campers.

This isn't to say that you have to sacrifice all your wishes when the family goes camping. Launching a trip way beyond the comfort, skill, and interest level of your young camping companions, though, drastically drops its chances of success.

Camping Keys

Keys to happy camping include staying warm and dry, when you want to; staying well fed, which you always want to; staying busy, even if it appears you're doing nothing worthwhile; and if you're a kid, getting wet or dirty or both, when you want to.

Where to Sleep

First, select a shelter. For many families, a large wall-type or big dome tent makes a lot more sense than a little backpacking tent. Tents seem to shrink drastically when family members tire, homesickness appears, or rain falls. Leave the backpack tent in the closet with the Led Zeppelin LPs for a few years. Buy a family-style tent, or at least rent one.

If the budget allows, get a dining fly, too, a tarp under which to cook, eat, or play games, whatever the weather.

For some kids, and some families, sleeping in a tent might be too big a first jump. A cabin-type camp might be better. KOA (Kampgrounds Of America) Kamping Kabins provide everything but bedding, food, and cooking gear. Many state parks and other camping systems also rent cabins. Another option is to rent a recreational vehicle (RV), such as a travel trailer or pop-up camper. Many dealers offer rentals.

(courtesy KOA)

Whatever the shelter, each person will need a sleeping bag and either a cot or sleeping pad for protection from the chilly ground. Invest in "three-season" sleeping bags, insulated well enough for all but cold-winter camping.

Campfires

Many camping memories simmer in meals and around campfires. Campfire etiquette has changed a bit, because campers in wilderness areas are now urged or even required to forego campfires and cook over small backpack stoves. That avoids burned rocks, destroyed topsoil, and other drawbacks of fires.

Most family campgrounds, happily, still have fire rings. The trick is feeding the fire. Chances are,

packs of campers have already scrounged every twig and log within hundreds of yards of the campsite. Vendors within parks, and nearby stores, often sell firewood, though. We visit a nearby sawmill and buy dry sawmill scrap for our campfires. We like to cook over the campfire, even though we prepare most meals on a Coleman gas camp stove.

Every adult knows how a fire should look, how often and in what way to tend it, and when to feed it more wood. The problem is, every kid camper has differing ideas on the same matters.

Teach campfire safety: clear a circle outside the ring, so the flames can't spread, use caution so that loose clothing can't catch fire, and clear away abandoned tools and toys so they don't trip someone passing by. Make the evening more pleasant for you and the child. Let 'em mess with the fire a bit, while you supervise.

Food

Plan food generously. Serve hearty meals and plenty of snacks for appetites awakened by outdoor activity. The kids can help with meals and clean-up. Let your young partners play a part, and not just on the "go-fer" errands. Let them stir the batter and flip the pancake. An error in cooking here doesn't seem as serious as at home. A little spill cleans up quickly with a bucket of water. Kids will quickly see why you try to cook more than one thing in the same pan, pack creatively to avoid waste and litter, and minimize the work. That's a good lesson in low-impact, environmentally friendly living that a family can take home.

All Dressed Up

There's no need for high fashion or several clothing changes per day. You do need variety, though. Cold seems colder outdoors; hot seems hotter. Pack layers of clothing, so that your campers can add or subtract layers to match ever-changing conditions. Temperatures are constant in our homes and schools; the great outdoors reminds us that things can change a lot and in a hurry.

Lots to Do

Parents like to loaf. Kids like to do stuff. Pack toys and tools. Consider fishing gear, swim fins, pie-makers, books, and toy characters that can turn a tent and sleeping bags into a wild universe and make camping more fun.

Plan nature hikes. Wandering through a natural area is a wonderful way to learn about the plants and animals with which we share Earth. A guide-book, a camera, a sketch pad, or a journal can record things you discover, to continue the learning process at home.

Kids shouldn't hike alone, any more than you'd send them for long walks solo at home. Don't overlook the dangers of getting lost. Buy a compass and learn to use it yourself from the instructions that come with it, then teach each kid how to find their way through nature.

People of all ages travel to learn about new areas and people. History makes that interesting, and campgrounds are often located near museums, monuments, and other historically significant areas. Visit some.

Swimming and camping are a perfect match. Pack swimsuits for all, and don't forget masks, snorkels, beach balls, and other water toys. If your family is going to camp, every member should learn to swim.

While thinking about safety, make sure to bring a first aid kit, insect repellent, sunscreen, and sunglasses.

Fishing is Fun

If your family will be fishing on its camping trip, keep it simple to keep it fun. Panfish swim closest to shore where you can cast to them. Spin-cast gear is most reasonably priced and simplest to use. Bait up with night crawlers or other worms (usually for sale near campgrounds) set a bobber to hold the bait just above the bottom, and try catch-ing your supper!

Most states don't require kids to have fishing licenses, but parents need them. If you're helping with the fishing, you probably need a license. Remember that license fees help create fishing opportunities. Ask for a rule booklet with the license. It will tell how you can fish, what you can catch, and what you can keep.

Bring on the Boats

Camping and boating go together well. If you don't own a boat to tow along with you, you might consider a canoe for a first family camping boat for rivers and small lakes. Some people hate a canoe's wobble. For them a folding boat might be better. Inflatable boats blow up quickly to provide a full-feature boat. Car-top aluminum boats, often 10 or 12 feet long, are traditional camping favorites.

At and near many parks you can rent canoes, fishing boats, or sailboats. It's a great chance to try out water sports before investing in them. Make it a family rule: everyone, parents and all, must wear personal flotation devices (life jackets) when on the water, and an adult should supervise all boating until kids prove their ability.

Campers love such outdoor games as Frisbee, badminton, soccer, and jump rope. Other lawn games pack well and provide hours of fun. Depend-ing upon the campground, bicycles may be the best gear you brought along.

Indoor Ideas

Camping is an outdoor pursuit, but there's considerable time spent indoors, too. Rain, day's end, fatigue, or boredom sends the young camper in the tent, and everyone's happier if he or she finds something pleasant to do there. Crayons and cards have saved many a family trip.

Reading's a natural. Fiction, nature guide books, and joke books are all good bets—joke books especially. Tents seem made for giggling in.

Writing seems easy when you're camping. There's lots that's new, and writing helps you remember it later. If you're on an extended camp-ing trip, post cards or letters to relatives or friends provide pleasure for writer and recipient. Write and tell them: Camping's a blast. It's a little different with the kids along, but they're having a ball and so are we.

You were a little afraid of camping with kids. But now that you've done it, gloat a little!

Sources

Bureau of Land Management
Department of Interior–MIB
1849 C Street Northwest
MS 5600/MIB
Washington, D.C. 20240
(202) 208–5717

Kampgrounds of America, Inc. (KOA)
P.O. Box 30558
Billings, MT 59114–0558
(406) 248–7444

National Park Service
1849 C Street
MS 1013
Washington, D.C. 20240
(202) 208–4747

U.S. Army Corps of Engineers
OCE Publications Depot
2803 52nd Ave.
Hyattsville, MD 20781–1102
(202) 761–0010

U.S. Fish and Wildlife Service
Public Affairs Office
1849 C. Street NW, Room 3445
Washington, D.C. 20240
(202) 208–5634

U.S. Forest Service
Public Affairs Office
P.O. Box 96090
Washington, D.C. 20090–6090
(202) 205–1760

Chapter 1
Camping Comfort Is in the Bag

Sleeping Bags

If there is one item of equipment common to camping in its many forms, from deep-wilderness to backyard campouts, it's the sleeping bag. Sure, you can create an old-fashioned bedroll from a pair of blankets cleverly folded together, but why?

Today's sleeping bags are better than ever before, and at prices that virtually anyone can afford. From $20 discount-store bags to high-tech specialty bags costing hundreds of dollars, you can match your needs and budget to a sleeping bag, and it won't keep you up at night!

Selecting a sleeping bag is quite simple. Decide how you'll use it: where you'll camp, and when. Then study fill materials, and factor in the shape of the bag, shell material, your budget, and a few other details.

Sleeping Bag Styles

Sleeping bags come in categories, with an understandable amount of overlap between them.

A four-season bag is designed for use in wilderness in harsh weather, where a sleeping bag can practically be a matter of life and death. As you might expect, these are expensive sleeping bags, often filled with down, which in turn is protected by a high-tech shell and lining and designed to provide maximum warmth at minimum weight, and

cost considerations are tossed to the wind. Few of us can afford a bag like this. Few of us need one.

A three-season backcountry bag is for the serious backpacker. It is usually filled with a quality synthetic material or down and designed to be as light as possible.

A car-camper bag is very affordable. Its weight and compressibility—ability to be squeezed into a small, light package—are not a consideration. Its low cost often is. These are the bags for sleep-overs and camping trips where the car is parked near the tent or camper. More of these bags are probably slept in each camping season than the other two categories combined. Most feature nylon linings and synthetic insulation.

Air is Essential

The most critical part of the sleeping bag is air. Moving air carries our body heat away quickly. It's the dead air locked into the bag and its fill that avoids this heat loss and keeps us warm. Sleeping bags, like articles of clothing, don't make us warm. They help us retain the warmth we create.

Sleeping bag fill comes in two main categories: down and synthetic.

Down, the insulating feathers grown by geese and other waterfowl, is the most expensive of sleeping bag and clothing insulators. Many say that pound per pound, it's also the warmest, lightest, most compressible, and most comfortable. It's hard to clean, though. And once it gets wet, it loses most of its loft, or dead air space, and thus most of its insulating value. A wet down bag in a harsh environment spells trouble.

Many good man-made or synthetic insulations have been developed. They come in three main categories: loose-fiber insulators and two types of quilted insulators.

Superior and most expensive are loose-fiber insulators, which behave and even look a lot like down fibers. These include the brands Primaloft, Lite Loft, and Micro-loft.

Thinsulate's Lite Loft delivers more warmth for its weight than any other synthetic on the market, according to Cascade Designs personnel. The company offers it in some sleeping bags. "Inch for inch," says Cascade Designs literature, "it even outperforms goose down."

A little bulkier are top-rated quilted insulators, woven fabrics of fibers, such as Polarguard and Polarguard II. Polarguard HV provides even more warmth for the dollar, according to Cascade Designs. Its polyester filament has a large hollow core.

Less expensive and a little bulkier yet are quilted insulators such as Hollofil and Quallofil.

A safe bet in comparing insulators is to compare price tags on the sleeping bags. The better the insulator, the higher the price. You're paying mostly for lightness and compressibility. That's why you should predict your sleeping bag uses and make sure you don't buy a lot more bag than you need.

Shell Game

Sleeping bag shells are made from many materials. Good, tough, light shell materials include rip-stop nylon, nylon taffeta, and polyester taffeta. More affordable but still serviceable for many campers is polyester.

Want to get really fancy? A new shell material called DryLoft from Gore, Inc., the makers of Gore-Tex fabric, breathes well and is waterproof. A sleeping bag made with Dry Loft costs about $100 more than the same bag in another material.

Sleeping bags come in many shapes; rectangular and mummy bags are the two extremes.

Rectangular and semi-rectangular bags are roomy, but they also have large empty spaces you need to keep warm with your own body heat, which makes them seem drafty. They're larger, too, so they weigh more than mummy bags made of the same material, and for that reason they're rejected by serious backpackers.

A mummy bag is more efficient, both in weight and heat retention, although many people feel too confined in them. The warmest bag of all is a mummy bag with a hood.

Want a compromise? Many bags are designed with features of each: a snugger fit than a rectangular bag, but with more tossing-and-turning room than a mummy offers.

Campers taller or shorter than average can even buy long or short bags to ensure that they don't carry too much bag or try to stuff too much body in too little bag.

How Cold?

Most sleeping bags are rated for the coldest temperature at which they provide comfortable sleep. In 1994 Cascade Designs built a Cold Environment Test Lab to precisely test insulation in sleeping bags and camping mattresses: A life-size multiple-temperature-zone test mannequin "sleepers" in sleeping bags while each bag's heat retention is measured.

Unfortunately, though, there's no industry standard on sleeping bag temperature ratings. One company's 30 degree bag might be a lot warmer than another's 30 degree bag. Neither of them might be as warm as you'd like for 30-degree camping. Ratings do give you an idea of the relative warmth-holding qualities of different bags. The advice of other campers you trust is a good factor to mix into your buying decision.

Still can't decide? Buy a bag you think might not be quite warm enough. You can wear long johns, add a blanket, or purchase a light liner to add comfort. Sleeping in a too-warm bag, at the other extreme, doesn't offer any options but unzip-

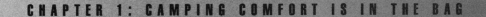

ping it completely, and that's seldom comfortable.

Just as there are differences in insulation and shells, there are various ways in which the insulation can be arranged.

Inexpensive bags sometimes have the insulating material stitched into place between the shell and liner fabric. That can provide plenty of insulating value in each tubular compartment, but practically none along the seams.

Sleeping bag makers have developed several ways to avoid this problem. Cascade Designs lock stitches its fiber layers to the shell and liner fabrics, then offsets them to form a continuous blanket with no "cold spots," areas where stitching between shell and liner offer an express route for warmth to escape.

Others use a shingle approach, in which multiple layers of insulation compartments overlap.

Better yet is a combination, in which a shingle system is combined with a single "floating" layer of insulation.

Products/Services

American Camper offers a full line of sleeping bags in three different insulations. Polycloud is a 100-percent non-allergenic polyester fiber the company calls perfect for three-season camping. DuPont Hollofil 808 is a hollow, warmer, polyester fiber. Hollofil II has multiple insulating chambers within its fibers. Most of American Camper's bags feature rectangular design; two exceptions are the Seminole, a hooded mummy bag with 3 pounds of Hollofil II and the Mohawk, a tapered hiking bag with 2½ pounds of Hollofil II.

B-West Outdoor Specialties offers four First Ascent sleeping bag styles, from its compact Tundra Down wall quilted bag ($249) to its rectangular down wall-quilted bag ($179–$319). The latter has a foot friendly zipper that allows the bottom section of the bag to be opened independently of the top.

Cabela's offers several sleeping bag models, including its top-of-the-line Arctic II Quallofil

($179–$184) expedition-style modified taper bags. The Arctic II, which comes in three models rated to below-zero sleeping, features shingle construction, with a "weather wedge" at the zipper start at the bottom of the bag, to keep cold out. It comes with a free fleece-lined stuff sack that converts into a pillow.

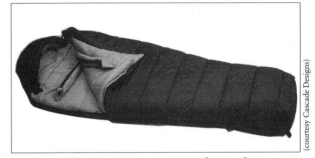

Cascade Designs Quantum 20°F sleeping bag

(courtesy Cascade Designs)

Cabela's Ultra Deluxe Adam & Eve sleeping bag

(courtesy Cabela's)

Cabela's Deluxe Woodsman sleeping bag

(courtesy Cabela's)

Cabela's Adam & Eve series of sleeping bags ($74–$199) are double bags with plenty of room for two. One of the bags holds 4 pounds of insulation, the other 3 pounds. Zip the two together, and arrange with either the 4 pound bag on top for cold nights, or the 3 pound bag on top for warmer ones.

Cabela's Deluxe Woodsman ($169–$249) sleeping bags come in three models, with comfort ratings as low as minus 40 degrees. The bags feature Quallofil insulation and a removable liner of Arctic Fleece. Double-layer offset construction in the bag keeps cold spots at bay. The rectangular bag, in three roomy configurations, has a heavy cotton duck outer shell.

Cabela's Deluxe Outfitter bag ($149–$164) is a classic, traditional sleeping bag filled with Quallofil and rated for temperatures down to minus 20 degrees Fahrenheit. The shell is made of tough, 10-ounce cotton duck. The bag's shape provides plenty of room.

Cascade Designs offers a variety of top-quality bags, with nearly all the best insulators and construction techniques represented, including dual five-layer shingle quilting, in which shingles of insulation are attached to a floating layer of insulation.

Cascade Designs has added some special features, such as a stash pocket inside the bag that can hold flashlight, glasses, or contact lens solution. A trapezoidal foot design lets feet take their normal, natural position, without loss of loft and warmth. Zippers are placed on top of the bag, where you can reach one when you need it.

Cascade Designs' Synergy bags are designed to

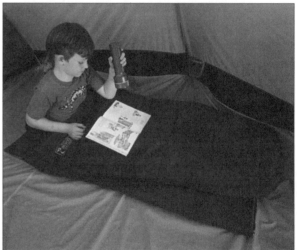

(courtesy Cascade Designs)

Cascade Designs Therm-A-Nest 30°F Junior sleeping bag

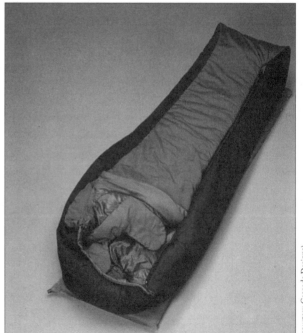

(courtesy Cascade Designs)

Cascade Designs Synergy 40 sleeping bag

Cascade Designs Quantum 20°F sleeping bag

accept a Therm-A-Rest pad (see description that follows), to provide an insulating base. That means you need less sleeping bag. You're buying less bag—and carrying less bag—because the Therm-A-Rest pad is doing some of the traditional sleeping bag's work.

Cascade Designs also crafts a novel approach to trail togetherness. The Therm-A-Nest bag can be used as a single bag, or mated with a second bag to create a sleeping bag for two. Better yet, it can be zipped to a Therm-a-Coupl'R sheet component, which holds two Therm-a-Rest pads to create a luxurious double bed at a minimum weight.

Quantum and Synergy bags by Cascade Designs have a "Fusion" hood, to contain the 40 percent of body heat said to be lost out the top of the head. A ZipSeal draft tube is sewn to press tightly against the zipper and avoid heat loss.

Coleman's wide line of sleeping bags—thirty-eight models in all—includes the new Coleman Double-Layer Comfort System, which features a two-layer bag with zip-in, zip-out fleece liner. Two bags in this system also feature special double-track zippers (parallel zippers for the bag and its liner). The Double Layer Comfort System includes a 4 pound Insul 33- by 77-inch tall bag, and a 4-pound Hollofil 808 39- by 80-inch king bag.

Also new from Coleman is a Center-Zip Bag, designed to make climbing in and out of the bag easier. It's available in a 3-pound Insul, 33- by 77-inch tall style. Coleman also offers two junior bags and standard sleeping bags for all four seasons in regular, tall, and king sizes. The line includes two double/van bags and two mummy-style bags, plus one tapered for cold weather use.

Fenwick makes three types of sleeping bags, all with outer shells selected for wind resistance, lightness, softness, and tear resistance. Linings are 100-percent polyester brushed knit. The bags are insulated with shingle-layered Polarguard HV, and other features include an insulated draft-resistant flap that stays snug against the zipper, a double-sided zipper for ventilation, and a compression sack.

Fenwick sleeping bags include 20 degree and 0

Coleman Center Zip sleeping bag

courtesy The Coleman Co.

degree mummy sleeping bags ($149–$199), 20 degree rectangular bags ($149–$159), plus a Z-Bag Multi-Degree Sleeping Bag ($159–$179) with three layers of insulation you can adjust to match varying weather conditions.

Jack Wolfskin premium sleeping bags include mummy and rectangular styles. The Arapahoe is a mummy bag with shingle construction and Thinsulate LiteLoft insulation. The goose down-filled Ascent offers more fill for wintry applications. The Dakota features triple-layer construction LiteLoft fill and a zippered foot section to match warmer conditions. The Papoose fits kids up to 4 feet 8 inches tall, and comes with a wolf hand puppet. It's filled with Hollofil.

Kelty sleeping bags ($60–$215) are made with Polarguard HV, Polarguard, and Hollofil II insulations, in both shingled and offset-quilt configurations.

The company's warmest bag, the Soft Touch minus 15 degrees HV ($215) has 58 to 62 ounces of Hoechst Celanese Polarguard IV insulation, shingled construction, and a hooded full-fitting mummy shape.

Women's bags offer 20 percent more insulation than non-gender bags, and are 6 inches shorter to cut excess weight.

For warm weather camping Kelty offers the Explorer 45° ($85) semi-rectangular bag, with 16 ounces of Polarguard HV fill, the semi-rectangular Nomad 55° ($75) with one side a single layer sheet for warm nights, the rectangular Le Tour 45° ($75) and Light Top 55° with its single layer top sheet.

Marmot sleeping bags($159–$689) are premium items, designed for mountain climbing and other technical applications. They're investments in dry, comfortable sleep.

Marmot ranks its down bags by fill power: the space one ounce of down takes up in a clear plastic tube. That's the "loft" or air space it provides for insulation.

Some Marmot bag shells are made of Pertex, a down-proof nylon material that is highly wind-proof and water repellent. Others are constructed with Gore DryLoft fabric, which provides a wind-proof, highly water repellent, breathable bag.

Marmot offers many options in its bags, including extra-wide models, ultralight bags, short lengths, right or left zippers, and custom overfills. Standard are features such as zipper draft tubes to seal against cold and a seven-section footbox to keep feet warmer.

Marmot's synthetic fill bags are made with Synsilk, a polyester fabric treated with Ultra Durable Water Repellent finish. Other fabrics are used in special purpose bags.

Traditional sleeping bags, Marmot says in its catalog, were made with either quilted or shingled layers of insulation. Each had good and bad attributes. Marmot's Dual Construction system places shingle insulation within a layer of quilted insulation compartments for the best of both.

Peak 1's line of twenty-one sleeping bags includes twenty new models. The Excursion Series of six bags ($95–$120) all feature temperature rat-

ings in the zero or minus 15 degree Fahrenheit range. Hollofil or Quallofil insulation is used in these mummy bags.

The Peak 1 Mountaineer Series ($125–$175) comes in three styles, each in regular and long lengths. Temperature ratings available in this series are zero, 15, and minus 15 degrees. The zero and 15 degree bags are insulated with Polarguard; the

Peak 1 Diamond Back sleeping bag / Adventure Series

minus-15 bag has Quallofil. The bags feature chest baffles, ground-level seams, insulated foot pockets, 3-inch insulated draft tube, and sculptured hood.

The Adventurer Series sleeping bags ($180–$215) include Peak 1's highest performance, most extreme weather condition bags. All feature Polarguard HV insulation, triple-layer top, and double-layer bottom. Other features include insulated foot pocket, chest baffle, double zipper guard, weather seal, and radially cut covers. Coldest rated is the Arrow Head, at minus 25 degrees, with 4 pounds of Polarguard HV.

Remington sleeping bags include several big, rectangular bags. The Caribou and Bighorn come in Realtree All-Purpose and Advantage camouflage covers, respectively. The Caribou is insulated with 5 pounds of Hollofil 808, for a 25 degree rating; the Bighorn has 6 pounds of fill for a rating of 20 degrees Fahrenheit.

The Remington Black Bear is an extra-long rectangular bag with 4 pounds of Hollofil; the Brown Bear is wide and long, with 5 pounds of Hollofil. The Whitetail is made for cabin, boat, or campsite sleeping. With a rating of 45 degrees, it is filled with 3 pounds of Hollofil. The Mule Deer has 4 pounds of fill and a rating of 40 degrees Fahrenheit.

The North Face makes premium, expedition-quality equipment, including a line of winter sleeping bags used by many mountaineers.

Goose down sleeping bags include the Inferno DryLoft ($695), the Solar Flare DryLoft ($515), the Foxfire DryLoft ($435), and the Ibex ($325). Another line of sleeping bags feature Polarguard insulation, Gore DryLoft shells, ThermaStat linings, and shingle construction. They include the Darkstar DryLoft ($455), Bigfoot DryLoft ($385), Snowshoe DryLoft ($335), and Cat's Meow DryLoft ($295).

Sleepgear: Pads

The concept is simple: a pad filled with foam for insulation against the ground, then with air for lofty comfort. From that concept sprang Cascade Designs' Therm-a-Rest, along with similar mattresses that followed.

Cascade Designs' founders Jim Lea and John Burroughs knew in 1971 that outdoor sleeping often offered both the proverbial rock and the hard place. Campers chose between closed-cell foam and air mattresses, neither of which alone delivered both warmth and cushioning. Lea and Burroughs combined the two, sealing foam within airtight covers and adding a valve. The Therm-A-Rest was

born, evolving into a practical and comfortable line of mattresses.

Therm-a-Rest mattresses ($50–$119) come in a variety of styles. From the Ultra Lite II ¾-length at 20 by 47 by 1 inches, with its insulating R-value of up to 2.7, to the luxurious EL Camp Rest Long at 25 by 77 by 2.5 inches and R-value up to 6.2, Therm-a-Rest shoppers can select size, loft, cover material, weight, and other features.

Therm-a-Rests continue to evolve. Company staff admit that some of the early models had cover materials so smooth a camper often slid off them in the night. So Cascade Designs and its mill found a way to bundle the material fibers and weave them "out of plane," for a texturized surface on which you can sleep tight. That material, Staytek, is available on several Therm-a-Rest models. Also new is Eco-Staytek with a fabric cover woven from polyester fibers made from recycled plastic soda bottles.

The LE (Luxury Edition) Therm-a-Rests have thicker foam, specially made so that the mattress is one-half-inch thicker at the same weight and rolled-up bulk as other models. They're covered with a stretch knit material with high friction to hold the sleeping bag in place.

Cascade Designs also has the Back Rest ($28), a lumbar pad that can be used anywhere, and the SportSeat ($19), a self-inflating Therm-a-Rest cushion.

Therm-A-Rest LE Camp Rest & LE Long camping mattresses

(courtesy Cascade Designs)

Therm-A-Rest'R Long Chair Kit

There are less expensive ways to sleep comfortably while camping, and Cascade Designs claims several of them, including its Ridge Rest closed-cell foam roll-up pads ($14–$28), and new Z-Rest fold-up "egg-carton" design pads ($23–$29).

Pad Tips from Cascade Designs:
- add an extra puff or two of air for loft, firmness; and
- store unrolled with valve open, because it will self-inflate faster.

Therm-a-Rest mattresses are the basis for Cascade's Therm-A-Rest'R chair systems. They feature stitched-in urethane wear strips to protect the precious mattress within. Chair Kits ($37–$62) are available in several styles, to match specific mattress models. One model comes with two removable closed-cell foam cushions, too.

Cascade Designs also makes Deluxe Pillows ($18–$24) filled with polyester and covered with soft fabric. They come with their own stuff sacks. Traveling light? The Pocket Pillow ($5) is a soft-fabric stuff sack in which your parka or extra clothing becomes the pillow fill.

American Camper offers three-quarter and full-

length self-inflating mattresses, each 1½ inches thick when inflated. The company also makes egg-crate and closed-cell polyethylene pads.

Appalachian Mountain Supply distributes Artiach self-inflating sleeping pads, including the Skin Mat, which it says is the lightest and most compact pad available. It features a non-slip polyurethane surface and comes in six model and size combinations. The Comfort Mat is slip resistant, with 100-percent textured polyester fabric.

Cabela's offers a Self-Inflating Sleeping Pad ($34–$46) with open-cell foam within an air-tight mattress inflated through a valve. It comes in three sizes.

Remington offers single-pillowed, straight-single, and full-size air mattresses, all made of canvas and a rubberized-blend material.

Quantum 0° sleeping bag with Therm-A-Rest'R Lite Chair Kit

Sources

American Camper
Nelson/Weather-Rite
P.O. Box 14488
Lenexa, KS 66285–4488
(913) 492–3200; Fax: (913) 492–8749

Appalachian Mountain Supply
731 Highland Ave., Northeast, Suite C
Atlanta, GA 30312
(800) 569–4110; Fax: (404) 653–0273

B-West Outdoor Specialties, Inc.
2425 North Huachuca
Tucson, AZ 85745
(520) 628–1990
Fax: (520) 628–3602

Cascade Designs
4000 First Avenue South
Seattle, WA 98134
(800) 531–9531
E-mail: www.cascadedesigns.com

The Coleman Company, Inc.
P.O. Box 2931
Wichita, KS 67201
(800) 835–3278

Fenwick
5242 Argosy Ave.
Huntington Beach, CA 92649

Jack Wolfskin
Johnson Worldwide Associates
Camping Division
1326 Willow Road
Sturtevant, WI 53177
(800) 848–3673; Fax: (414) 884–1703
E-mail: camping@racine.jwa.com

Kelty, Inc.
113-B Industrial Drive
New Haven, MO 63068
(800) 423–2320
E-mail: supertioga@aol.com
Web site: www.kelty.com

Marmot
2321 Circadian Way
Santa Rosa, CA 95407
(707) 544–4590
E-mail: Info@Marmot.com
Web site: www.Marmot.com

Peak 1
P.O. Box 2931
Wichita, KS 67201
(800) 835–3278

Remington
Nelson/Weather-Rite
P.O. Box 14488
Lenexa, KS 66285–4488
(800) 255–6061; Fax: (913) 492–8749

The North Face
2013 Farallon Drive
San Leandro, CA 94577
(800) 447–2333

Chapter 2
Tents: Gimme Shelter

Tent Tenets

Four questions face the camper considering purchase of a tent: how big, how light, how weatherproof, and how much? Increase size and weatherproofness, slice weight, and you drive up the price. One more consideration is design: dome, or A-frame.

A-frame or tunnel-shape tents are lightest, at least partly because they don't contain as much living area. If sleeping is your sole concern, or weight considerations outweigh other concerns, the tunnel is for you. Most of us, staying closer to the trail head and fearful of bad weather and close living, go for the dome, which offers headroom and good ventilation, and can be set up without stakes if necessary.

Tents are rated by how many bodies can sleep in them. Remember, that's how many bodies of average size can be laid next to each other until the floor of the tent is covered. Most of us don't want to live or camp that way. Buying a tent one size larger can pay big comfort dividends, unless you're on an absolute ounces diet.

There are three-season and four-season tents. Unless you're going to camp right through the winter, a three-season tent is plenty strong, and much lighter than its year-round counterpart.

Backpack Tents

A backpacker has special tent needs. It must be light, watertight, and rugged. For a quick overnight camp for two people, a tent as heavy as 8 pounds can be used, experts say. For a longer trip the tent should weigh less than 6 pounds; if the trip is long and three or four people will be using the tent, it should still weigh less than 9 pounds.

A vestibule, or covering for one end of the tent, makes it much easier to stash wet boots, packs, or other items outdoors.

The happiest campers I know use a tent rated larger than their actual needs. Two people survive foul weather much more successfully in a three- or four-person tent than in a traditional two-man. They find other ways to cut pack weight to make up for the difference.

Well Grounded

A ground cloth serves two purposes: It keeps moisture off the tent floor, which is not always waterproof, and it protects it from rocks and other objects. A sheet of thin plastic cut in the shape of the tent, but an inch or two smaller, works on smooth ground. A heavier ground cloth is needed where it's rocky or rough. The ground cloth should never extend beyond the tent walls, or it will actually funnel water under the tent.

Material Matters

Coleman, a maker of tents as well as all kinds of camping equipment, says most tents are made of nylon, which is strong, lightweight, water-repellent when coated, and colorful. For most family camping, bathtub-style floors with factory-sealed seams are important for weather protection, and a rain fly provides additional rain and storm proofing. "Ventilation and ease of set-up are important considerations, too," the company says.

Products/Services

B-West Outdoor Specialties offers instant pop-up shelters and tents from Africa, all made of 100 percent polyester waterproofed with an acrylic coating. Each of the African Legends products use a figure-eight frame to replace conventional poles. You simply remove the coiled frame, with the inner tent attached, from the carry bag, and it sets itself up. You then add the fly. The Instant Pitch Sunshade Cabana ($49–$169) provides sun and wind protection. Tents ($109–$349) come in several models and sizes.

B-West also offers large Sunseeker canvas tents,

from an external frame Dome ($699) that sleeps five to the Villa ($1,399) that offers an external frame, large veranda, and two private sleeping compartments with a separate living area.

Bass Pro Shops' Sunrise III 2-Room Cabin Tent ($199) is a 10- by 16-foot design with a center divider to create two 8- by 10-foot rooms. Center height is 6 feet 10 inches. Large "no-see-um" windows on all four walls provide ventilation. The Sunrise III comes with an awning for shade and rain protection. It sleeps up to 10 campers.

The Lake Home Screen Tent Combo ($179–$219) from Bass Pro Shops also features a 6- by 9-foot screened area adjacent to the high-walled main tent that has four windows for ventilation. The tent comes in two sizes: a 9- by 9-foot for four or five campers, and a 12- by 10-foot that sleeps eight.

Bibler Tents says it makes not only the finest, lightest, and most stormproof tents possible but the only single-walled, completely waterproof tents. Escalante three-season tents feature a three-layer waterproof and breathable laminated fabric, freestanding design, and two large doors for ventilation. Each door is covered by a built-in freestanding vestibule. A stormproof top vent sheds rain and lets out warm, moist air, but can be rolled back for star viewing. The vestibules also roll up to increase ventilation.

Poles on the Escalante tents, which include the two-person Piñon and three-person Juniper, are the same shock-corded aluminum poles used in Bibler four-season tents.

In Bibler's four-season tent line, the I-Tent was originally designed for the extreme mountain climber, but at 3 pounds, 10 ounces and room for two, it was quickly appreciated by other outdoor travelers. The Eldorado is similar, but 5 inches longer and 3 inches wider. The Kiva follows the same design ideas, but sleeps four while weighing just over 6 pounds.

Bibler's line includes several other models of free-standing and hoop design tents.

Journal Entry July 21, 1988: Last Night, I Slept in a Tent

I spent last night in a tent. That's not big news, I suppose, but it came as something of a shock to me. I'd slept in plenty of tents, from Boy Scout lean-tos to family tents, from New Hampshire mountains to Washington state steelhead riverbanks. I'd frozen in tents on the Ontario shoreline of Lake Superior and sweltered on Lake Michigan's Manitou Islands.

South Manitou Island is more civilized than its sister to the north. Here the ferry pulls up to a dock, National Park Service rangers welcome you, and a little store sells a few supplies plus chili, hot dogs, and hot dogs with chili. You pick out a campground destination, shoulder your backpack, and head out.

If your wife is six months pregnant, carrying within her a rapidly growing first child, the tent has shrunk since the last camping trip, and now barely clears her belly. About the time you remember its low price (who needs a rain fly, anyway?) the clouds darken, and the skies begin to weep. The sky cries for the next thirty-six hours, and you try to read, play cards, find an unbruised piece of your body to lay on the hard ground, and shoo cowpoke hungry and shelter-seeking mosquitoes out the door and down the not-so-dusty trail.

The ferry is to return at 10 A.M. on the third day of your stay. The little store opens at 7 A.M. You spend three hours eating chili, hot dogs, and hot dogs with chili, all the while watching water ooze out of your packed gear.

The first tent in our family was a big canvas wall tent, pitched at a large state park in north-central Lower Michigan for a week or two each summer. It was there that I first learned about flat air mattresses and army surplus sleeping bags from which the pointed stems of down (chicken feathers, actually) would poke the occupant.

I learned about the hazards of mildew, which required the canvas house to be re-erected in the backyard if a dew so much as kissed it within twenty-four hours of striking camp.

Anything more than a dewy kiss was likely to enter the tent, too, if not from the sides or roof, then from the bottom. So, as the Boy Scout manual dictated in those days before Earth Day and environmental awareness, we'd chop a trench around the base of the tent to carry away the worst of any downpour.

If there's one vision of a Boy Scout tent that will remain with me forever, though, it was the one pitched perfectly, just a few feet too close to a campfire ring. A troop mate was visiting a neighbor's tent when he noticed his dingy green home-away-from-home had turned orange. He stood with hands clutching his face, his feet glued to the forest floor, muttering simply, elegantly, over and over, "My tent!"

I was old enough to know better a dozen or so years later when I pitched a tent in a hollow along Brook Trail in New Hampshire's White Mountains. Of course it rained that night. Sleeping bags don't float. Four-pound sleeping bags weigh more than that when rain-soaked and lugged downhill. It was all pure learning experience and on a honeymoon, yet.

Not all my tenting memories are traumatic. From a tent in South Dakota's Black Hills I once counted six different shades of blue clouds as a summer storm tumbled out of the mountains. I once sat in a tent, motorcycle parked nearby, and ate bare-handed a New York strip steak brought to my camp by a girlfriend after her shift at a restaurant. I married her.

And now daughter Elizabeth is closing in on three years of age. She wants to camp, mainly because she wants to hold a live frog in her hands. As good a reason as any to camp, I suppose.

Last night, July 20, 1988, I slept in a tent. It didn't rain. It didn't snow. Fire never threatened the structure, and mosquitoes weren't much of a problem. Some would call that a normal night's camping. I know better. We just got off easy.

American Camper has added a new compact, lightweight backpacker tent, the Ultra-lite ($44) to its full line of tents. The new tent sleeps one, and measures 6 feet 10 inches by 4 feet. It has a rain-resistant, nylon-taffeta roof and heavy-duty tub-

For sleeping or playing, it's hard to beat a tent.

Lake Home Screen Tent Combo

(courtesy Bass Pro Shops)

style floor. It weighs 3½ pounds and is 17½ inches long when rolled up.

Each American Camper tent is set up and inspected at the factory and covered by a three-year warranty. Each features Durawrap P-2000 shock-corded poles, which is a polyester weave laminated around fiberglass poles. Tents range from the Ultra-lite to a large 18- by 9-foot Shenandoah three-room cabin.

Cabela's Alaskan Guide model is a modified geodesic tent designed to take plenty of abuse from the weather. A shock-corded six-pole system supports the tent of 100 percent ripstop nylon, with a floor made of abrasion-resistant oxford nylon. The rainfly sheds both rain and snow, and extends over the door to protect against sunlight and precipitation. The D-design door can be half-opened for ventilation without letting in rain and snow.

It comes in four- ($249), six- ($299), and eight-person ($369) models. An optional vestibule ($49–$54) provides storage for bulky items.

Camp Trails, well known for its packs, now makes backpacking and family tents for the price-conscious consumer. Joining the line recently were the Starlight and Moon Shadow series. Both feature good breathability, excellent fly coverage, teardrop window design, and spacious interiors. Floors are bathtub-style to provide protection from wet ground.

The Starlight series ($79–$179) offers two- to ten-person models. Moon Shadow tents ($139–$259) sleep from three to six people.

Coleman has added eight tent designs to its line, upping its total to twenty-four models.

Leading the way is the Guide Series, a line of rugged tents that range from the 7-foot square. Vagabond I and 9-foot square Vagabond II domes with full length rain flies and vestibules, to the 15- by 7-foot three-room Dakota.

The Dakota also offers full-length fly, awning, multiple guylines, and factory-sealed, coated nylon-oxford, puncture-resistant floor. Each of the six tents in the Guide Series features large windows and doors, interior mesh storage compartments, nylon coil zippers, and Coleman's No-See-Um mesh screening. Each tent's storage bag has set-up instructions sewn in.

Other Coleman tent offerings include the A-Frame/Dome Series with six styles from the 9- by 7-foot A-Frame Mountaineer IV to the 10-foot square five-person Deluxe Country Lodge. Coleman also offers seven models in the popular cabin-style-tent design.

For campers on the go, Coleman offers three two-person Ultralight tents, including the Bivy Tent, Ultralight II, and Mountaineer II. Beyond tents, the company also offers a 10-foot square Portable Picnic Shelter and an 11-foot square Dining Shelter.

Eureka!, a mainstay of the camping tent market, has introduced several new models featuring the company's new High/Low Climate Control door system. It's available on fourteen Eureka! models, including several entry-level tents. The design allows the camper to open the bottom of the door to let in more cool air. For less cool air, open the door from the top so cooler airflow remains close to the ceiling. The system was developed and tested for U.S. military missions in the Arctic, jungle, and desert environments.

Eureka!'s original umbrella-style tent is now available in a new series called the Equidome ($169–$369), offering campers an aluminum frame tent with luxury features at a moderate price. The self-supporting Equidome tents have durable four-pole frames, with a spider center fitting. Shock-corded poles and clips make set up speedy, and the tents feature full-fly coverage. They're available in two- to six-person models.

The new Mountain Pass tent ($189–$269) has a canted fly and door, and the High/Low Climate Control Door System. The three- to four-season backpacking tent comes in two-person (5 pounds 8 ounces) and four-person (8 pounds 8 ounces) models.

Eureka! also has a full line of four-season tents ($269–$379), which stand up to harsh weather in any environment. They feature StormShield Plus 75-denier ripstop polyester flies, roofs of 70-denier ripstop nylon, floors of 1.9 ounce taffeta nylon,

and poles of 7000-series aircraft aluminum.

Eureka!'s backpacking tents ($89–$379) are compact and light, with several ultalights weighing less than 6 pounds. The new Solitaire ($89) features a bivy-style shape, a fiberglass frame, a net roof for star gazing, and a folded size of just 4 by 18 inches. The Timberline ($149–$209) remains a backpacking classic. The original self-supporting A-frame tent sets up quickly.

Eureka! family tents ($139–$889) are spacious, well-ventilated, and set up quickly and easily. They feature 1.9-ounce permeable nylon for roofs which let moisture escape beneath the rain fly; 1.9 ounce taffeta nylon in top flies, walls and floors; and frames of seamless aluminum or fiberglass, depending on model.

Jack Wolfskin tents are made in one- to four-person models, all with anodized aluminum, shock-corded frames. Roof vents and door openings can be adjusted to control the rate of ventilation to match the camping conditions. Floor, walls, and fly are made of ripstop polyester. All seams are double stitched and factory sealed.

The new Devil's Tower from Jack Wolfskin is a two-person tent that weighs 5 pounds 13 ounces. A full-fly version is available for four-season use. The 2-pound 13-ounce Soloist is a compact lightweight tent for the cyclist or lone camper.

Kelty has introduced a vaulted design to its tents to combine simple set up with superb ventilation. Poles still slide through a single sleeve, to make set up easy, while the sleeves are attached to the tent with spacers to separate the tent and rainfly for best ventilation.

Kelty offers a full line of tents with aluminum ($180–$320) or fiberglass ($130–$420) poles, sleeping up to six people.

Kelty expedition tents including the Windfoil ($550–$650) are narrow aerodynamic lightweight tents that can be set up by one person in two minutes.

Marmot tents are built for durability, habitability, and field repairability, according to company staff. Tents have pole stabilizers and internal

Journal Entry June 2, 1991: Revenge of the Cheap Screen House

Ever since the first cave visitor decided that camping would go better with an adjustable fire, waist-high table, and a sleeping area lined with saber-toothed tiger fur, each camper has tried to go it one better.

The result sulks at my feet.

It is a screen house. The box says it is. The lady who sold it says it is. It is a cheap screen house. My wife, who bought it at a rummage sale, admits it is.

I almost dodged this nylon and aluminum bullet. Wife brought the thing home in a box, I shoved it into the forbidden zone between garage rafters and garage roof. It seemed the perfect place for this alleged screen house.

And so it was, for a long time. "We should try it," my wife said, several times. She hates mosquitoes. They love her. She dreams of a campsite where bugs of prey rattle against a screen while she *nah-nah-nah-nah-nah-nahs* them from a bug-free picnic table, novel in hand.

She remembered the screen house on the eve of a camping trip. Nothing would do but to tug the boxed creature from its raftery repose and try setting it up in the yard. The box slid across the two-by-fours, pushed by a cracked canoe paddle, and I braced myself for the catch. There was no strain. It was a truly lightweight screen house. Much lighter than one would have been with poles.

Poles?

The picture on the box showed poles. The box held none. I then stuck the thing back overhead.

Fast forward, now, two years. The same lady has another rummage sale. My wife recognizes the place and asks if someone ever stumbled across an extra bundle of aluminum poles. The lady blushes, deeply. She tells her sons to check at the cabin that weekend. A few days later she calls. Pole city!

Today, I packed for another camping trip. I pulled down the light box with the light house.

Six hours later, I found the bundle of poles. Six hours later yet, one hundred miles down the road, I'm sitting at a picnic table, bugs flying about my face, gas lantern drawing fresh insect recruits, and the screen house sulking in a sniveling heap.

A cheap screen house has the shape and consistency of a jellyfish, only a million times larger. Instead of tentacles it has poles. Dozens of them, it seems, that all hook together somehow although the picture on the box doesn't clearly show how, to form a skeleton for this nylon animal.

To erect the monster you must hold all thirty-seven poles at the same time. Your arms must stretch 8 feet in each direction, your teeth grip the center, your feet secure the corners, your eyes anticipate the last effort of the creature to break the hold.

A cheap tent house is sure to defeat you. It sheds one pole bone with a clank, then snickers in nylon talk. You can wait for more aluminum pole bones to fall; I prefer to throw them, myself.

I kicked, and cursed camping and rummage sales and, especially, cheap screen houses.

"Why do you think people sell these things at rummage sales?" I asked my wife. She didn't answer. She thinks people sell things like cheap screen houses because the items have brought them pleasure and they wish to share that joy.

You can't even make fun of someone with a heart that pure. If you're not an outright cad, you'll buy her a proper screen house—a quality structure like those we describe here—and then share the bug-free picnic table with her.

(courtesy Cabela's)

Cabela's Alaskan Guide Model modified geodesic tent with optional vestibule

(courtesy Johnson Worldwide Associates)

Camp Trails Moon Shadow tent

(courtesy The Coleman Company)

Coleman Guide Series Dakota tent

guy systems to spread pressure among poles, floor, and body. Steep walls increase headroom, D-shape doors don't drag on the ground, and pockets and gear lofts provide for convenient storage. All tents have a spare parts kit and instructions.

Marmot's double wall tents—the two-person Nutshell ($289), Peapod ($325), and Bastille ($469), and two- to three-person Citadel ($525)—provide increased living room. They feature a continuous mesh sleeve and clip combination for maximum headroom and easy set up. The Citadel also features a pole-supported vestibule that can be used as a kitchen or closet.

Single-wall tents are made for those who want to move fast and light. Marmot offers the Taku ($599) and Asylum ($525), both two-person tents. They're built especially for those camping on

mountain climbs.

Nelson Weather-Rite's Cool-Breez ($159) is a dual-purpose, 10-foot square screen house–sun shelter combination, with insectproof-mesh side walls. Walls can also be easily slid to corner points and secured to the interior of the leg. Roof and corner pieces are constructed of a resilient polyethylene fabric that resists fading, tearing, mold, mildew, and over-stretching. Its powder-coated, chain-corded frame has nylon corner and peak joints.

Peak 1, a Coleman division, recently re-entered the backpack tent field after a seven-year absence, with four new models. All feature strong, light, shock-corded anodized aluminum poles, durable shock cords, reinforced corners, tub floors with factory-sealed seams, and lapfeld-stitched seams, which are interlocked doubled-fabric with double-stitching. Also included are full-length rain flies with factory-sealed seams. Generous zipper cuffs on doors, windows, and vestibule openings provide superior weather protection. The rain fly stretches over the entire tent, extending out past the doors to create a vestibule to keep gear dry.

The Peak 1 Orion tent ($185) is a two-person, rectangular dome tent with a double vestibule and a total of more than 21 square feet of coverage for gear. It has two large doors and two large mesh panels. On clear nights you can leave the rainfly off

(courtesy Johnson Worldwide Associates)

Eureka! Mountain Pass 2

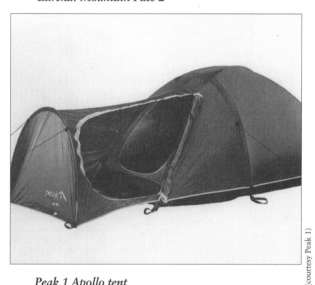

(courtesy Peak 1)

Peak 1 Apollo tent

(courtesy Bass Pro Shops)

RedHead Sportiva Ultimate Dome Tent

for fresh air and star viewing. In foul weather, seal the vestibules closed with Velcro patches. Mesh gear loft and storage pockets provide storage for small items.

The Apollo ($220) weighs 6 pounds, and stands tunnel-shaped at 7 feet 9 inches by 4 feet 10 inches. The Triton ($160) weighs 4 pounds 8 ounces, and provides a 7-foot 6-inch by 4 foot 4-inch shelter with 38-inch center height. The Talon ($250) is a three-pole dome tent with two large D-doors. It measures 7 feet 9 inches by 4 feet 9 inches with a 48-inch center height.

RedHead's new Village Dome Tent ($199) is a

two-room design with a 12- by 9½-foot overall floor area, separated by a zippered room divider. Center height is a generous 83 inches. The roof of poly/canvas does not require a rainfly.

RedHead's new Pine Lodge 3-Room Combo Cabin ($299) tent has three 6- by 11-foot rooms within its 18- by 11-foot dome, with zippered dividers. Center height is 80 inches. Entry is through a D-style door, and two large hooded windows provide ventilation plus protection from rain and sun. Durawrap fiberglass roof poles are shock-corded, and quick-clips speed set-up and tear-down. The floor is rugged polyethylene, and nylon walls are coated.

RedHead's Sportiva Ultimate Dome Tents ($199–$249) feature a screened porch attached to a 10-foot square tent that sleeps six, or a 12-foot square model that sleeps eight.

Remington tents by Nelson/Weather-Rite include two new models and a gazebo. All are Quick-Set tents, made of 800 mm polyurethane-coated nylon taffeta, with floors of 265-gram poly-ethylene. A Quick-Set Hub System provides assembly in just minutes, thanks to a hub with num-bered, locking outlets that are easily matched to numbered tent poles. Hub and corner pieces stay affixed to the tent or gazebo.

The Remington Quick-Set Two-Room Cabin Tent ($234) sleeps six, with a base size of 12- by 9-feet and a center height of 80 inches. It features an easy access D-style door. The door window and three large side windows let air in and keep bugs out.

The Quick-Set Screen-Cabin Tent Combo ($189) sleeps four and offers a large screen room as part of the structure.

The Quick-Set Screened Gazebo ($209) has the same measurements as the two tents and provides a bug-proof environment for outdoor activities.

The North Face makes high-end outdoor equipment, including tents for mountaineering and backpacking. The company invented flexible tent poles in the early 1970s and later the first geodesic dome tent.

Mountaineers have cherished the North Face's VE-25 ($645) for its 20-year history. The classic tent has stood on K-2 and Mount Everest more times than any other tent, according to company staff.

The North Face's lightweight single-wall tents are completely waterproof, eliminating the need for a rain fly. They include the 48-square-foot Apogee-24 ($850), 44.3-square-foot Tempest-23 ($675), and 30-square-feet Assault-22 ($525). The company also makes a line of premium three-season tents.

The ultimate tent? Perhaps it's The North Face's 2 Meter Dome ($5,000), a 136-square-foot geodesic dome that sleeps up to ten people, and allows several to stand fully upright. It has served as a communications tent, medical tent, and living shelter on many expeditions.

Sources

American Camper
Nelson/Weather–Rite
P.O. Box 14488
Lenexa, KS 66285–4488
(913) 492–3200; Fax: (913) 492–8749

B-West Outdoor Specialties, Inc.
2425 North Huachuca
Tucson, AZ 85745
(520) 628–1990; Fax: (520) 628–3602

Bass Pro Shops
1935 South Campbell
Springfield, MO 65898
(800) BASS–PRO

Bibler Tents
5441–D Western Ave.
Boulder, CO 80301
(303) 449–7351

Cabela's
Department 9BA–50M
Sidney, NE 69160
(800) 331–3454

Camp Trails
Johnson Worldwide Associates
Camping Division
1326 Willow Road
Sturtevant, WI 53177
(800) 848–3673
Fax: (414) 884–1703
E-mail: camping@racine.jwa.com

The Coleman Co., Inc.
P.O. Box 2931
Wichita, KS 67201
(800) 835–3278

Eureka!
Johnson Worldwide Associates
Camping Division
1326 Willow Road
Sturtevant, WI 53177
(800) 848–3673
Fax: (414) 884–1703
E-mail: camping@racine.jwa.com

Jack Wolfskin
Johnson Worldwide Associates
Camping Division
1326 Willow Road
Sturtevant, WI 53177
(800) 848–3673
Fax: (414) 884–1703
E-mail: camping@racine.jwa.com

Kelty, Inc.
113-B Industrial Drive
New Haven, MO 63068
(800) 423–2320
E-mail: supertioga@aol.com
Web site: www.kelty.com

Marmot
2321 Circadian Way
Santa Rosa, CA 95407
(707) 544–4590
E-mail: Info@Marmot.com
Web site: www.Marmot.com

Nelson/Weather-Rite
P.O. Box 14488
Lenexa, KS 66285–4488
(913) 492–3200
Fax: (913) 492–8749

Peak 1
P.O. Box 2931
Wichita, KS 67201
(800) 835–3278

RedHead
Bass Pro Shops
1935 South Campbell
Springfield, MO 65898
(800) BASS–PRO

Remington
Nelson/Weather-Rite
P.O. Box 14488
Lenexa, KS 66285–4488
(913) 492–3200
Fax: (913) 492–8749

The North Face
2013 Farallon Drive
San Leandro, CA 94577
(800) 447–2333

Chapter 3
Backpacking

If the thrill of camping comes from feeling at home in the wild, then backpacking must be the biggest thrill of all. For not only are you providing all your own equipment and know-how, you're carrying all you need on your back.

It heightens the satisfaction to know that you're ultimately responsible for your own well-being on the trail. Twist an ankle, forget the compass, pitch the tent in a hollow; you're on your own to work it out. Completing a backpacking outing successfully means you know how to take care of yourself.

Backpack Basics

John Johnson is a friend who has backpacked all over North America. He often has his family in tow, and has learned how to pursue this form of camping so economically and efficiently that he teaches a course on it at our local community center.

Johnson tells his students that there are many things to like and dislike about backpacking. Pluses are the often wonderful fishing, photography, day hikes, wildlife observations, swimming, berry picking, and rock collecting the backpacker enjoys. Tradeoffs can include bears and other animal nuisances, high-altitude problems, mosquitoes, black flies, horse flies, snakes, and other people. Most of

the drawbacks can be avoided or dealt with so that the positives can be savored.

Big questions in planning a backpacking trip are how long you will be "out," and how far you will hike. The answers depend on your tastes, as well as your age and physical shape. If in any doubt about your physical condition, check with a doctor

Dayhikes can carry campers to stirring sights.

One payoff for backpackers is beautiful views.

before heading out. Remember that help may be days or miles away.

Johnson advises that beginners start with day hikes of 1 to 4 miles allowing one to four hours for a peaceful pace with plenty of time to enjoy the surroundings.

Some people like to plan long, fast day hikes with light loads. They can cover 10 to 20 miles in four to eight hours.

An overnight backpacking trip might include a hike of 1 to 10 miles. You can take on this trail with an inexpensive sleeping bag and boots, and a 30- to 40-pound pack.

A long weekend backpack trip might cover 10 miles to 30 miles in two to three days. You need light equipment and food, and that costs more. Your pack will be in the 40-pound class.

An extended backpacking trip, 10 to 60 miles, more than three to six days, calls for advanced skills and gear: a light tent, mountaineering clothing, high-tech sleeping bag, medium-weight boots, and freeze-dried foods in a pack weighing as much as 50 pounds.

Johnson suggests picking a backpacking destination by first browsing through guidebooks, many

of which are available at public libraries. Bookstores and camping equipment stores also stock these books. Select a park or other area, and write to it for details on regulations, reservations, opportunities, maps, and related material. Start well in advance. Topography maps aren't often needed for most backpacking trips. Simpler maps provided by the parks are usually sufficient, and easier for casual campers to follow.

Preparing to Backpack

Johnson advises a training program to prepare for long backpacking trips. Try a year-round approach including three one-half-hour aerobic workouts each week, plus two weight-lifting or Nautilus workouts each week. For aerobic workouts that mix fun with work, try cross-country skiing, hiking, or walking in the woods, jogging in the woods on a grass surface, canoeing, roller skiing, bicycling, or swimming.

Trail Tips

Many backpacking problems can be avoided

Journal Entry: From the Beaver Slide to the Moose Crossing

"I started at the beaver slide and fished down almost to the moose crossing," Dale Smith said, explaining where he'd caught the 5-pound steelhead trout.

Had the fish been caught elsewhere, Dale might have described a river stretch from an old car tire to a power line. The fish might have been larger, but the experience could not have been fuller. An 8-mile hike, pack on back, had paid off. The steep hills and nervous river crossings had proven entrances rather than obstacles. The Lake Superior shoreline wasn't so much cold and deserted as it was peaceful and inspiring. And the steelhead fishing within Lake Superior Provincial Park was, in a word, superior.

Several rivers race through the park on their way to Lake Superior, tumbling over waterfalls and pausing only slightly before finishing their whitewater journey. Up those rivers swim bright, slim, rainbow trout—steelhead—bent on reproducing.

A few hours after we'd pitched our backpack tents. I watched a pot of coffee perk while my companions thrashed the Lake Superior "surf" with a variety of spoons. Dale finally cast into a pool where the river made a final pause before shooting into the big water. A steelhead followed his lure but did not strike, and that drew my interest away from the river-water-based coffee to my spinning rod.

I tossed a heavy spoon into the pool, and a few minutes later a 4-pound steelie was safely tethered to a stringer, and the evening menu had switched from a freeze-dried turkey tetrazzini to trout, rubbed well with margarine, wrapped in heavy foil, and baked twenty minutes per side over a medium wood fire.

Dale wandered upstream and, a few hours later, returned with another fish, this one caught near the moose crossing. The next day others took over. George Roberts, celebrating his retirement from a carmaker career with his son Mike, caught the first steelhead of his fishing career, an 8-pound beauty, then added a trophy-size brook trout of about 18 inches.

Other prizes of the trip were memories: a seat on a rock overlooking a falls, pans and cutlery scrubbed clean with sand, a moose visible a second or two before it scooted back into thick brush, and scarlet-cheeked steelhead trout caught in this this land of beaver slides and moose crossings.

by planning ahead and heading out prepared, according to the **American Hiking Society** (AHS), which represents more than half a million outdoors enthusiasts.

Carry a map and compass, and know how to use them. Dress correctly for the anticipated weather and be prepared for changes. Wear the right shoes or boots for the trail. Don't hike alone or in groups too large. Bring a fully stocked first-aid kit and extra food. Make sure you drink only safe water. Guard against sunburn and heat exhaustion. Be careful crossing streams. Avoid snakes, poisonous plants, and poisonous insects.

AHS says backpackers should make sure their gear includes the basics: proper footgear, extra socks, long-sleeve shirt or jacket, hat, canteen, extra food, sunglasses and sunscreen, insect repellent, first-aid kit, flashlight with fresh batteries, map and compass, waterproof matches, knife, raingear, and plastic garbage bag.

Gathering the Gear

Backpacking tents are covered in Chapter 2. Smart, seasoned backpackers add an extra rainfly to their gear. That provides a separate shelter for cooking, especially wise and welcome in bear country where you shouldn't cook in the tent or near it. It's a separate shelter, too, when it rains, and offers a place to relax and read. Doubling your protected living space is a godsend when the weather sours. Rainflies are light and can be stretched over a rope strung between a couple of trees.

Backpacking sleeping bags are covered in Chapter 1, and boots and other clothing considerations in Chapter 6. Another big concern is something you can't carry enough of with you.

Water!

Backpackers are almost always thinking about water. Hiking with a pack on your back increases sweat, and replacing lost fluids is key to good health as well as good times.

But water is heavy; about 8 pounds a gallon. It's almost impossible to carry enough for more than an overnight backpacking trip, especially if you're counting on freeze-dried foods, to which water must be added in the cooking process.

Trailside water taps are scarce, which means the backpacker often collects water along the way. Contaminated water is both a short- and long-term health hazard.

Water Hazards

Pathogens, or harmful organisms, come in three categories, according to the staff of SweetWater, maker of water filters and purifiers.

Protozoa are the largest water-borne pathogens, at 1 to 16 microns, a unit of measure 1 millionth of a meter long. You can see things 50 microns and larger. Protozoa cause such legendary camping maladies as *Giardia* (beaver fever) and *cryptosporidium*. They're not bothered much by chemical treatment but can be filtered out quite efficiently.

Bacteria are intermediate size organisms, at 0.2 to 10 microns. They include *E. coli, Virbrio cholera, Salmonella*, and others. Disinfectant chem-

icals tame them, and they'll be caught by any filter proven to remove 99.9999 percent of bacteria.

Viruses include rotavirus, Hepatitis A, Norwalk, polio, and others. They're tiny, 0.02 to 0.085 microns. That makes them difficult to filter, although they respond well to chemical disinfection.

Dangers

The effects of drinking bad water can be seen in hours to months. Typical complaints include fever, cramps, fatigue, diarrhea, nausea, dehydration and other symptoms, varying slightly with the malady. None are pleasant and, in some people, water-borne illness can be fatal. How common is the danger? Ninety percent of the surface water in the U.S. fails to meet U.S. Environmental Protection Agency's standards for acceptable drinking water, according to SweetWater. It's worse elsewhere.

Campers rightly fear *Giardia*. About one-third of us seem resistant, but the remainder can suffer chronic diarrhea, cramps, bloating, frequent stools, fatigue, and weight loss. Filtering and boiling appear the best defense, although chemical disinfection works if the chemicals are left working for longer than normal time periods.

Giardia has long been a top concern of wilderness visitors. Now some experts say the infectious protozoa *Cryptosporidium* outranks *Giardia* as the top waterborne threat in the outdoors.

People whose immune systems are already suppressed are placed especially at risk by "*Crypto*." It led to more than one hundred deaths when it broke out within Milwaukee's municipal water system in 1993. More than 87 percent of surface water in the country is thought to be contaminated with *Crypto*, according to SweetWater.

Treatments

Chemical disinfection, with iodine or chlorine crystals, does not remove *Crypto* from the water, and even *Giardia* may be inactivated only after the chemicals are left working even longer than manufacturers advise.

Obviously, there's a payoff in avoiding water problems.

From the standpoint of pathogens there are four main ways to make water from springs, lakes, or rivers safe.

Boiling water for a full minute (some experts recommend 10 minutes), then letting it cool to room temperature, kills or inactivates all pathogens. If you're backpacking in the mountains, at elevations of more than 6,562 feet, let it boil an extra two minutes. Safe doesn't necessarily mean tasty; boiled water tastes flat. A vigorous stirring helps.

Chemical disinfectants such as iodine and chlorine kill or inactivate bacteria and viruses, although they're not quite as reliable where protozoa are the problem. They leave a taste some people dislike, require reaction time, take much longer in cold water, and pose worry for some people with chemical allergies. Iodine is generally reported more effective than chlorine.

Filters remove bacteria and protozoa—the threats of *Giardia* and *Crypto*—but not viruses. Matched to a carbon element, they also trim inorganic contaminants, tastes, and odors.

Purification protects against all three pathogen culprit categories. Purifiers are regulated by the U.S. Food and Drug Administration. They're the best bet in crowded areas where sanitation systems may be overworked, or where people aren't observing good hygiene practices. They're the device of choice when you aren't willing to take a chance on your water.

For most backpackers, a filter will do the job, because viruses occur mainly in more settled areas where human fecal matter contaminates the water you're going to drink. If in doubt, step up to a purifier, or get that water boiling. Just remember that boiling requires fuel, which is another fluid to lug along.

Filters become clogged when they catch the stuff you don't want to drink. When they do, you have two choices. Clean the filter, or replace it.

Make sure when you shop that you can do one or the other easily and in the field, far from a workshop. A clogged and uncleanable or unreplaceable filter is worse than none at all; you've lugged it along, after all, and may not have made other provisions to chemically treat or boil water!

Water Products/Services

SweetWater calls its new WalkAbout Microfilter "the best $35 filter in the world."

It offers total protection against *Giardia*, *Cryptosporidium*, and bacteria, using the same Labyrinth Depth Filter technology to capture bacteria and protozoa as does the Guardian Microfilter.

The WalkAbout is 6.5 inches high, and weighs just 8.5 ounces, with all accessories. It offers one-step filter cleaning in the field, with lightweight replacement filters available at about $12.50. The WalkAbout offers a pumping speed of 0.7 liter per minute.

Many filters are soon stopped by silt. You can't see chunks of stuff in the water if they're smaller than 50 microns, but your filter may be able to catch pieces $\frac{1}{50}$ of that size! In no time, your filter can be full of them.

SweetWater's new Silt Stopper ($9.95), can be used with any portable water filter or purifier where water quality is a little cloudy such as in sediment-rich run-off waters, lakes filled with algae,

Guardian+Plus water purifier from SweetWater

Cabela's Water Bottle fanny pack

and waters otherwise contaminated. The Silt Stopper catches larger contaminants before they reach your main filter. It measures about 2 by 2 inches, and weighs less than 1 ounce. It can be back flushed when clogged, and filters can be replaced (three-packs, $8.95).

The SweetWater Guardian+Plus Portable Water Purifier ($72) is said to be the only product on the market to eliminate *Giardia*, *Crypto*, bacteria, and virus. It also has a built-in carbon bed to remove any strong iodine taste.

It weighs 15 ounces and has what the company describes as an easy-to-use design that allows for simple field maintenance and ergonomic pumping. It has a flow rate of 0.7 liters per minute.

The Guardian+Plus meets all Environmental Protection Agency purifier standards for total protection against unsafe water. It works in three stages: Water first passes through an iodinated resin bed (removable if you're in pristine areas); the water then enters the Guardian Filter Cartridge, and is pumped out through the Labyrinth Depth

Filter, removing *Giardia, Crypto,* bacteria, and other parasites and worms; lastly it enters a packed bed of granular activated carbon. The carbon removes all but trace amounts of residual iodine and absorbs other chemical pollutants, odors, and flavors.

A Backpack Primer

Most full-size packs have a frame system to give them form and help distribute the load. Most can be described as *external* or *internal* frame packs.

External frame packs have visible frame members, often made of aluminum or plastic. They're best for carrying heavy loads, and excel on smooth, gradually sloped trails. When adjusting an external frame pack make sure its hip pad rides on your hips, and that no part of the frame touches your back. The pack should be loaded with the weight as high in the pack as possible.

Internal frame packs have frame members inside the pack bag, sometimes in fabric pockets. They're best for travel over rough, steep terrain, because their lower center of gravity offers better balance. They also free the shoulders and arms for the movements necessary in skiing, climbing, and similar activities. Many have a single pocket, rather than the multiple pockets often available in external frame packs, and thus pose more challenge when organizing gear. For smooth-trail travel, pack the weight high in an internal frame pack; for rough country pack it lower, closer to your center of gravity.

Stays, the frame members of internal packs, are contained in fabric pockets. Kelty, a top pack maker, said the stays are designed to fit the bodies of most backpackers, but need to be removed and adjusted to match the camper's body. Mark the area that's proven uncomfortable when backpacking, and remove and gently bend the stay to match the body contour better.

The beauty of a vertical stay system is that the frame doesn't interfere with the movement of

(courtesy Cabela's)

Cabela's Forest Alaskan Pack

(courtesy Cabela's)

shoulders when hiking, skiing, or reaching for something, such as an anchor spot when climbing.

Whichever pack style you choose, you can pack clothing and other items in plastic garbage bags to protect them.

Backpack Products/Services

American Camper has introduced a new line of internal frame backpacks, the Voyager, Bighorn II, and Pioneer. Each carries a lifetime warranty.

All three packs are constructed of 420 High-Density II nylon packcloth, which has a double-pass coating to provide extra protection from harsh elements. Each also has internal lightweight aluminum stays that can be removed and adjusted to a backpacker's back.

The panel-loading Voyager ($59–$64) has a large front zippered pocket inside a main compartment, a padded yoke to protect the back from the frame, two large front and two large side pockets, and a front accessory pocket.

Camp Trails Scirocco pack

(courtesy Johnson Worldwide Associates)

The top-loading Bighorn II ($69–$79) has load leveler and anti-sway hip adjustment straps, adjustable contoured shoulder straps, a zip-open divider that separates the main bag from the lower compartment, and nylon-webbing accessory loops for equipment.

The top-loading Pioneer ($59–$64) features two large interior compartments, a drawstring cordlock closure at the top, large top pocket within the lid, two small open hip pockets, and an ice ax or accessory loop.

B-West Outdoor Specialties offers camping equipment from Africa, including the Alpine ($149–$189) and Trekking ($129–$229) series Back-Packer R.S.A. packs. These rucksacks feature harness systems with quick and easy adjustments, adjustable internal frames of lightweight aircraft aluminum, pack bodies made of strong and abrasive-resistant Duracore, nylon-spiral YKK zippers, and DuPont Delrin Acetal buckles. Four different harness systems are available.

B-West also features internal frame daypacks and hiking rucksacks ($59–$79) in its Back-Packer line.

Cabela's extensive backpack line includes the Forest Alaskan III pack ($149–$159 with frame), with a removable divider, 17-inch side pocket, and back side slip pocket. Two smaller pockets and an expandable pocket on the back all add up to 4,600 square inches of space. Hidden padded backstraps convert it to a daypack. As a full backpack, its lightweight aluminum frame has padded full S-curve shoulder straps, and a deluxe hip belt.

Cabela's also offers its Water Bottle Fanny Pack ($42), which provides storage for maps, snacks, extra clothing and a water bottle in a camouflage-pattern fanny pack; and its Deluxe White-tail Day Pack ($59–$64), available in camouflage or Blaze Orange, and made of quiet soft Polartuff material.

Camp Trails' new Triad series ($99–$109) internal frame packs have a thermoformed back with ventilation channels and a polyester tricot outer layer for comfort even when wearing the pack without a shirt. The internal, tubular aluminum frame is S-shaped to curve in at the bottom and direct the pack's weight to the hip area.

Camp Trails expanded its internal frame pack line with the Scirocco series ($49–$79) that fit children, teenagers, and short-waisted adults, particularly women. The packs range in size from 2,140 to 3,480 cubic inches. The larger two packs feature stabilizing straps on shoulder straps and hip belt, and an adjustable sternum strap to maintain a snug fit.

Camp Trails' full line of backpacks includes external frame packs featuring the company's V-truss, limiting corner-to-corner diagonal stress, with four crossbars for added stability. Other external frame packs have the ComfortFlex frame, molded from a single piece of high-impact copolymer polypropylene, to flex with you as you walk.

The company also offers a wide selection of daypacks and other packs. The Side Trip is a handy expandable fanny pack with two side waterbottle pockets. The pockets can be removed to leave just the pack or be worn alone on a belt.

Coleman Daysack

(courtesy The Coleman Company)

Coleman has introduced an angled zipper on its daysacks, daypacks, and backpacks to keep cargo in place even when the bag is unzipped.

Coleman offers four daypacks, all made of 420-denier nylon pack cloth with 1,000-denier bottoms, ranging in capacity from 1,910 to 2,165 cubic inches. They feature a mesh-covered, quilted, and foam-padded back panel; side reinforcement wings; internally taped seams; double-stitching at all zipper and stress points; and a pocket organizer with key clip.

Three different styles of backpacks are in the Coleman line, including a new frameless backpack-style for short hikes or overnight stays. Capacity of the frameless backpacks range from 2,400 to 2,935 cubic inches.

Hikers and mountain climbers who prefer internal frame backpacks can select from three

Coleman models. Each features a parallel, internal aluminum alloy frame; compression straps; contour shoulder straps with adjustable sternum strap; and padded hip belt with lumbar pad. The capacities range from 2,670 to 4,710 cubic inches.

To carry more gear, especially over well developed trails, Coleman external frame backpacks hold from 3,500 to 5,424 cubic inches of gear and offer aluminum alloy external frames and clevis pin attachments.

Eagle Creek daypacks feature DuPont Cordura-Plus nylon, protective padded backs, double-thick padded shoulder straps, heavy duty zippers, reinforced stress points, storm flap covers, double-needle zipper construction, taped seams, and lifetime warranties.

Eagle Creek's Backcountry series includes day pack and trek packs, alpine rucksack, and the Backcountry Guide Pack, an internal frame pack with a capacity of 2,800 cubic inches.

Backcountry waist packs include the Backcountry Baha, with a roomy main compartment, insulated water bottle holsters, additional pockets and panels, and lumbar support panel.

Eureka! recently expanded its line to offer both internal and external frame backpacks. The Raven, Eagle, and Talon external frame backpacks feature Eureka!'s Contour-Form frame that is designed to fit the natural contours of a person's back and reduce side-to-side sway. Each of the three packs is shaped like a person's back—wide across the shoulders and narrow at the hips—so the weight is carried on the hips.

Frames in the external frame backpacks are made with ⅞-inch aluminum, coated with an enamel-like finish that resists scratching, chipping, and corrosion. The strong frame is lighter and more durable than traditional frames, the company says.

The Raven ($149) has a capacity of up to 3,710 cubic inches, the Eagle ($179) up to 5,330 cubic inches, and the Talon ($219) up to 5,300 cubic inches. All have packs made of 420-denier ripstop pack cloth with two main compartments, full-length side pocket, wrap-around front com-

pression straps; and zippered security pocket inside the top compartment.

Eureka's internal frame pack line has been expanded to include an all-purpose backpack and several new rucksacks ($69–$99). Rucksacks are ideal, company staff say, for overnight trips with light to medium loads—and are especially good for skiing, snowshoeing, climbing, biking, hiking, or camping.

The new Nova backpack ($259) has a narrow, streamlined design, two compartments accessed

(courtesy Johnson Worldwide Associates)

Eureka! Talon external frame pack

(courtesy Johnson Worldwide Associates)

Eureka! Nova pack

through the top, a detachable fanny pack and mesh water-bottle pockets for day hikes, vertical and horizontal compression straps, and a capacity of up to 5,360 cubic inches.

Fenwick's Outdoor Performance Gear backpacks include the Weekender ($149) and Weeklong ($199) models, each made with high-density 420 denier nylon oxford to be strong, durable, and tear- and water-resistant. Shoulder straps are custom molded, and hip belts are padded. The Weekender has a 3,594 cubic inch capacity; the Weeklong 5,816 cubic inches.

Fieldline makes duffel bags, backpacks, fanny packs, gaiters, and other equipment.

SeamLock construction features pack shoulder straps sewn directly into the main pack body seam, reinforced with extra strong seatbelt webbing. Seven layers of material are sewn together and anchored with four bartacks.

The Fieldline line includes daypacks and fanny packs, and combinations so the fanny pack can be removed for quick side trips.

Granite Gear's line of internal frame backpacks include the Precipice Alpine Mountaineering Pack and the Cornice Ski Mountaineering Pack. Frames are made with high-density polyethylene, ½-inch closed-cell foam, and one aluminum stay. The frames are all contained within a nylon sheath. The newly designed belt has an external skeleton of recycled plastic with a hip-bone cup, dual-density foam belt, and Spandura sheath. The Precipice holds 3,300 to 3,700 cubic inches, depending on model, and the Cornice holds 2,800 to 3,200 cubic inches.

The Couloir Back-Country Day Pack is a mid-size pack for overnight backcountry ski trips. It holds 2,400 to 2,600 cubic inches of gear. The Arête Summit Pack is a modern version of the classic top-loading rucksack, say company personnel, and the Crux Summit Pack resembles it, but without the Arête's front compression flap.

Granite Gear's Aurora Day Pack rides on the hips like a well designed technical pack.

Other Granite Gear packs include the

Yosemite backpack

Hydrolizer Water Bottle Hip Pack, which comes with two 20-ounce water bottles, and the Nighthawk and Falcon hip packs, among others.

Jack Wolfskin internal frame backpacks are made with ripstop ArmaTech fabric that not only resists punctures and abrasions but stops rips through a grid reinforcement system.

Jack Wolfskin offers several suspension systems, including the ACS (Air Circulation System) a flexible, perforated plate, with a mesh screen stretched over it. It comes with the Moonwalker climbing or dayhike pack, or the Salvation weekend or trekking bag. The Lightback carrying system offers the HDPE (high-density polyethylene) framesheet, which can be used for full loads, or removed for day hikes and lighter loads. It comes on four pack models. The Alpha suspension system features a soft breathable mesh wrapped around a perforated closed-cell foam pad. At the top of the line is the Alpha Plus suspension system, included in the new Pingora, an expedition pack with up to 6,280 cubic inches of capacity.

JanSport is a pack specialist, beginning with the patented flexible aluminum frame it introduced in 1967. JanSport pack innovations continue.

Technical internal frame packs feature JanSport's Stable Load Comfort Suspension System (as do all the company's technical packs). Other features include shoulder pads of dual density foam and C-cut design curves around the body to distribute load and shoulder pressure evenly. A stable load hip belt made of multi-density foam padding and contoured to rest on your hips provides positive load transfer. A microgrip lumbar pad provides firm lower back support. Pack capacity ranges from 5,200 to 6,350 cubic inches depending on the model.

The company's internal frame packs all feature RipCord, an exclusive JanSport fabric, made of 500-denier Cordura yarn, reinforced with 1,000-denier yarns woven in a ripstop pattern. A 1-ounce polyurethane coating provides waterproofing.

External frame packs from JanSport have aluminum frames that offer both strength and "give" for comfort. They range from 2,495 to 6,750 cubic inches in capacity.

JanSport's Yosemite and Nepali packs transfer the load of the frame directly to the hips with an exclusive hip arm made of Zytel. Push-button adjustments allow changes of position of the hip arm.

JanSport daypacks feature heavyweight fabrics and zippers, double-stitching, and reinforcement in areas that endure high stress. The new Sole series has molded, patent-pending waterproof rubber bottoms.

Many daypacks are designed more for town and campus than for camping. For real outdoor adventures, however, the JanSport Dayhiker offers a padded Coolguard mesh for comfort and ventilation, an ice ax loop, lashing square, lashing loops, and two front pockets for quart-sized water bottles.

The water-resistant Cross-Country daypack offers padded back and shoulder pads, compression straps, lashing loops, and storm flaps.

Moving up in size, the Mountaineer, Little Tahoma, Tahoma and Super Sack carry heavier loads. The Alpine Pack is bigger yet, 26 by 13½ by 11¾ inches, with specialty features such as a hinged front pocket to stow avalanche shovels and snowshoes, wide straps to secure a snowboard, and mesh side pockets for water bottles.

On a smaller scale, JanSport offers several fanny packs, including some that hold two quart-sized water bottles each for long hikes.

Kelty made its first backpack in 1952, long before the sport achieved widespread popularity. It has remained an industry leader as the sport has blossomed. Long a maker of external frame backpacks, the company was also an early entry in the internal pack field with its Tour Pack launched in 1973.

Among Kelty's new internal frame packs are three models that feature its LockDown suspension system, with shoulder straps, back pad, and load lifter straps mounted on a stiffened panel that slides up and down on the frame to match the torso length of the pack wearer. The shoulder straps are locked down on the sides by wide Velcro fasteners.

A SlabPocket within Kelty internal packs makes it easier to pack the densest gear close to the back to carry it most comfortably. Items in it, such as heavy food, water, stove, and so on, can be reached through the opening at the top of the pack, or from a GoferHole on the suspension side, behind the wearer's head.

Kelty packs offering the LockDown, SlabPocket, and GoferHole features include the Slickrock ($200), Zuni ($200) for women, and LaSal ($225).

The Radial Light XLT ($200) is Kelty's flagship external frame pack, with up to 5,535 cubic inches of volume, radial frame, curved shoulder straps with load lifter, and a telescoping frame which adjusts to match the wearer and load.

The Women's Tioga ($145) features narrower shoulder straps, a more conically flared waist belt,

Mountainsmith MountainLight series packs

(courtesy Mountainsmith)

Peak 1 Modoc backpack

(courtesy Peak 1)

tested in some of the world's toughest locations, including Mount Everest and Mount McKinley.

Items in the Mountainsmith line are modular so the latest accessories and upgrades will fit on older Mountainsmith products.

New in the Mountainsmith line are Mountain-Light lightweight expedition backpacks ($95–$395), designed for the advanced mountaineer. The company calls them the lightest full-featured expedition packs in the world. Mountainsmith women's expedition packs ($246–$395) include three models tailored to match the female anatomy.

Mountainsmith's Lumbar Series is called the world's No. 1 waist pack; its patented suspension system adjusts to precisely match individual anatomical differences. The packs also feature the company's high-comfort torso-hugging OmniBelt, carrying loads of up to 35 pounds without shoulder straps. They include new mesh side water bottle pockets.

Peak 1, a Coleman company, has added four new internal frame backpacks and one frameless pack to its lineup.

The Peak 1 Coronado is an internal frame pack with Stash pockets on both sides that can either carry plenty of gear or be tucked behind zippers when not needed. Compression straps on side pockets snug down loads. The top load bag has a spacious hood compartment, and the hood detaches to become a fanny pack. The Coronado offers 4,980 cubic inches of volume. Like all Peak 1 internal frame packs, it has a 600-denier polyester body with 1,000-denier nylon bottom, internally taped seams, aluminum stays, and many other features.

The Shoshone is a dual compartment top loader, with 4,620 cubic inches of storage. The biggest Peak 1 internal frame pack is the Modoc, a 5,110-cubic-inch dual compartment pack with a bottom compartment big enough to hold a sleeping bag. The Gunnison is a panel loading pack, with 3,475 cubic inches of storage.

For day trips or light overnight duty, Peak 1's Bridger is a frameless backpack with a capacity of

and a lowered packbag to create a more stable and more comfortable pack for women.

Kelty also offers daypacks and fanny packs.

Mountainsmith specializes in high quality U.S.-made backpacks, cycling packs, and outdoor and adventure equipment. Its high performance gear is

2,410 cubic inches. It features a large front pocket with mesh outer pouch for grab-quick items.

Peak 1 external frame packs feature the company's Next Generation Frame, made of an advanced composite material reinforced with Kevlar to increase strength and reduce weight. The tough frame weighs just 2 pounds but provides both vertical rigidity and torsional flex.

The Ocala pack is a dual-compartment top-loader offering 4,325 cubic inches of storage. The Oconee is similar but boasts a capacity of 4,805 cubic inches.

Rap-A-Pak offers a pack that converts into a ground cloth or work area. Designed especially for rock climbers and other outdoor enthusiasts, the Rap-A-Pak was designed by rock climber Larry Bordine and his wife Nancy. The pack, made of 420-denier urethane-coated nylon, features a padded back support, three compression straps, and shoulder straps. It unfolds into a 46- by 72-inch ground cloth.

Remington packs from Nelson/Weather-Rite include an external frame pack with 3,600 cubic inches of storage within its heavy duty nylon oxford, which is polyurethane coated. Included is a zip-out center divider and six zippered outside pockets. The pack frame is made from tubular aircraft aluminum and is anatomically S-curved.

The Pinnacle internal frame backpack has removal aluminum stays that can be adjusted to fit the curve of the wearer's back. The suspension is adjustable to fit any body shape, and the pack features contoured shoulder straps. Total volume is 5,250 cubic inches.

Remington daypacks and rucksacks are made of Cordura Plus Deluxe 1,000-denier material and are bar-tack stitched at all high-stress points. They feature large main compartments and YKK zipper closures.

The North Face backpack line is made for mountaineering, rock climbing, and serious back country travel. It includes seven series of packs.

The Alpha Series features strong, lightweight materials; ergonomically molded components; and an effective load transfer strut that the staff say makes the Alpha the most advanced internal frame packs ever made. Micro-Fit Series packs are made for extended backpacking and backcountry ski trips. Backcountry Series packs feature clean lightweight suspensions, and durable construction.

Tech Packs are specialty packs for rock climbing, two-day alpine climbs, and summit attempts. Ski and snowboard packs are also specialty packs. Day packs are compact and compartmentalized. Lumbar packs are designed for day hiking.

The North Face's Day Pack line has been expanded. All have double-stitched seams bound with bias tape inside the pack. Most feature foam-padded back panels, organizer pockets, key clips, oversized YKK zippers, and tough, abrasion-resistant fabrics.

The Tenaya ($55), with 1,700 cubic inches of storage, features a front pocket that allows the wearer to stash clothing without opening the main compartment. The Tuolumne ($44) at 1,500 cubic inches, has side pockets for water bottles. The Mohave ($49) now offers mesh water-bottle pockets the wearer can reach while hiking.

Sources

American Camper
Nelson/Weather–Rite
P.O. Box 14488
Lenexa, KS 66285–4488
(913) 492–3200
Fax: (913) 492–8749

American Hiking Society
P.O. Box 20160
Washington, D.C. 20041–2160
(301) 565–6704
Fax: (301) 565–6714

B-West Outdoor Specialties, Inc.
2425 North Huachuca
Tucson, AZ 85745
(520) 628–1990
Fax: (520) 628–3602

Camp Trails
Johnson Worldwide Associates
Camping Division
1326 Willow Road
Sturtevant, WI 53177
(800) 848–3673
Fax: (414) 884–1703
E-mail: camping@racine.jwa.com

The Coleman Co., Inc.
P.O. Box 2931
Wichita, KS 67201
(800) 835–3278

Eagle Creek
1740 LaCosta Meadows Drive
San Marcos, CA 92126–5106
(619) 471–7600
Fax: (619) 471–2536

Eureka!
Johnson Worldwide Associates
Camping Division
1326 Willow Road
Sturtevant, WI 53177
(800) 848–3673
Fax: (414) 884–1703

Fenwick
5242 Argosy Ave.
Huntington Beach, CA 92649

Fieldline
1919 Vineburn Ave.
Los Angeles, CA 90032
(213) 226–0830
Fax: (213) 226–0831

Granite Gear
P.O. Box 278 Industrial Park
Two Harbors, MN 55616
(218) 834–6157
Fax: (218) 834–5545

Jack Wolfskin
Johnson Worldwide Associates
Camping Division
1326 Willow Road
Sturtevant, WI 53177
(800) 848–3673
Fax: (414) 884–1703
E-mail: camping@racine.jwa.com

JanSport
N850 City Highway CB
P.O. Box 1817
Appleton, WI 54913–1817
(800) 558–3600
Web site: www.jansport/com

Kelty, Inc.
113–B Industrial Drive
New Haven, MO 63068
(800) 423–2320
E-mail: supertioga@aol.com
Web site: www.kelty.com

Mountainsmith
18301 West Colfax Ave.
Golden, CO 80401
(800) 426–4075

Peak 1
P.O. Box 2931
Wichita, KS 67201
(800) 835–3278

Rap-A-Pak
302 West 12th Street
Traverse City, MI 49684
(616) 922–3481

Remington
Nelson/Weather–Rite
P.O. Box 14488
Lenexa, KS 66285–4488
(800) 255–6061
Fax: (913) 492–8749

SweetWater
2505 Trade Centre
Suite D
Longmont, CO 80503
(800) 55–SWEET (557–9338)
Web site: www.sweet-h2o.com/sweetwater

The North Face
2013 Farallon Drive
San Leandro, CA 94577
(800) 447–2333

Chapter 4
Family Camping

*W*hat separates family camping from backpacking? Mostly, it's how much gear you can take, and that's because of how you get it there. Family campers usually travel by car, truck, or van, and they usually like the convenience of handy camping gear—coolers, cook stoves, tables, cots—equipment that lets them enjoy primitive surroundings without living in privation.

In other chapters we look at sleeping bags (Chapter 1), tents (Chapter 2), and cooking (Chapter 8). Here we're going to discuss some of the other items available to make family outings more enjoyable.

Products/Services

All-Luminum Products is one of the world's largest producers of camping furniture, according to the company. Its One Piece Picnic Table & Bench Set features a molded plastic tabletop and bench seats, with heavy-duty aluminum frame and steel bench supports. The company's Aluminum Cooking Table stands on 1-inch tubular aluminum legs, as does its Aluminum Top Table that seats six people and folds in half for easy storage and carrying. Several other camping and tailgating tables are available, including one-piece, drop-leaf, and centerfold models.

All-Luminum also makes Aluminum Director

Chairs, folding Sun'n'Sport and Fishing Chairs, and aluminum frame fold-away cots and beds, including one bed that can be used as an adjustable three-position padded recliner chaise by day. The company also offers the Rio Beach Collection of beach chairs and umbrellas.

American Camper offers the Easy Light double-mantle deluxe propane lantern, which uses piezoelectricity to ignite without matches. The double mantles produce 600 candlepower of illumination, burning six hours at the maximum setting with a 16.4-ounce propane fuel cylinder. The company also offers a standard double-mantle lantern, and deluxe and standard single-mantle lanterns.

Accessories from American Camper include lantern bags, propane hoses, and refillable tanks. A full selection of camping tools includes axes, folding shovels, machetes, and folding saws.

Portable furniture makes a campsite more comfortable. American Camper sells folding stools and chairs, folding cots, stowaway tables, and hammocks and hammock supports.

Browning's line of Ballistic Lites flashlights can keep campers out of the dark. Each is submersible to at least 500 feet, made with high impact ABS housing, Lexan lens, and built-in battery shock protection system. Xenon powered spot beams are more than 400 percent brighter than ordinary flashlights. They range from the 6-inch, 6-ounce 25 mm Micro to the 60,000 candlepower Afterburner.

Buck Knives' BuckLights family of hand-held flashlights are bright and waterproof. They range from the BuckBrite, just 3 inches long and featuring a key ring, to a four-C-cell model. Five models feature ABS plastic bodies, and are waterproof to 500 feet. Pre-focused, integrated lamp-reflector units throw a long, true bright beam.

Cabela's Gazebo ($199) lets in fresh air but keeps out bugs, harsh sunlight, and rain. It measures 13 by 15 feet at its base, with screen panels and a 210-denier taffeta nylon roof. A Sportiva hub provides quick set-up. An optional and removable fly/awning ($119) closes in the shelter for weather protection and privacy.

There never seems to be enough room in the camping car so Cabela's offers its Roof Top Carrier ($149). It attaches to a luggage rack, or to the roof with a Universal Mounting Kit ($14). The car-rier itself is made of heavy duty, ultraviolet-resistant vinyl, with three adjustable compression straps to cinch down odd-shaped loads.

Cascade Designs makes it easy to get excited about a towel: its Packtowl. What's so special about the Packtowl? Well, camping can be a damp activity and the soft Packtowl even absorbs water when the towel is wet. Made of 100-percent Viscose, it picks up as much as nine times its weight in water, then wrings out 90 percent of it to go back to work. Instead of wearing out, it gets softer and more flannel-like with each washing. The company's staff advise against drying in a clothes dryer but it air-dries in minutes.

Packtowls come in three sizes, from 10- by 27-inch ($6) to 20- by 40-inch ($13).

Cascade Designs also purchased Tracks, a manufacturer of hiking and walking staffs, in 1990. Expanding that line, they now offer six different models of hiking staffs.

Coleman has a long and wide line of top quality family camping gear, but its image, and indeed

Cabela's Gazebo

(courtesy Cabela's)

Cabela's Roof Top Carrier

(courtesy Cabela's)

Coleman Model 2000 NorthStar lantern

(courtesy The Coleman Company)

All Kinds of Camping

The United States offers about 16,000 public and private campgrounds. There are about 8,500 privately owned campgrounds, located near national parks and forests, popular tourist attractions, and in cities and small towns. Many, say Recreation Vehicle Industry Association personnel are themselves vacation destinations, with swimming pools, playgrounds, convenience stores, and other features.

Camp-resorts are usually open year-round and offer activities such as tennis, racquetball, miniature golf, swimming, fishing, saunas, and fitness clubs. Some offer condominium investment opportunities. There are currently nearly 500 RV camp-resorts in the U.S.

Kampgrounds of America (KOA) was established in Billings, Montana, in 1962. The industry leader in franchised family campgrounds now offers more than 75,000 campsites at hundreds of locations throughout North America and abroad.

Almost half of KOA campgrounds are open year-round, and most are within 100 miles of large communities. Known especially for their RV facilities, many KOA campgrounds also have Tent Villages, which offer tent campers covered cooking and eating areas, running water and electricity, lockable storage cabinets, and private, grassy tent sites.

KOA has made the link between the computer and the great outdoors. KOA Kyberspace puts every KOA Kampground at your fingertips, on the company's World Wide Web home page: http://www.koakampgrounds.com/.

Selections on the home page menu include basics such as Who is KOA, and What to do at KOA, plus directories of rates, features, and locations of specific KOA Kampgrounds. You can place an order for a KOA directory, road atlas, or camping guide.

KOA Kamping Kabins offer the security and comfort of a log cabin with lockable door and wood-frame bed with mattress. All you need is bedding, cooking and eating utensils, and personal items. There are always rest rooms, hot showers, and coin laundry facilities nearby. Kamping Kabins come in two sizes: one room, for up to four adults; and two room, for up to six adults.

The 367 U.S. National Parks contain more than 440 campgrounds with more than 29,000 campsites.

There are more than 4,000 campgrounds in 156 of the U.S. Department of Agriculture's national forests.

The Bureau of Land Management, part of the U.S. Department of the Interior, manages 270 million acres of Western U.S. lands, with plenty of camping opportunities.

U.S. Army Corps of Engineers projects offer more than 53,000 campsites near oceans, rivers, and lakes.

National Wildlife Refuges, created to offer refuge to wildlife, sometimes offer camping opportunities, too. They're described in *National Wildlife Refuges—A Visitor's Guide,* available from the U.S. Fish and Wildlife Service.

Parks operated by state and local governments offer many camping opportunities, too. To learn more about them, contact the chamber of commerce or travel bureau in the area you'll be visiting.

its logo, is linked to the gas camping lantern. Recently, that venerated lantern was updated.

The new NorthStar Model 2000 lantern ($99) is the company's brightest ever, with many features sure to make it popular with campers everywhere.

What makes the new lantern special? Light. Lots of it. Twenty percent more light than the Powerhouse lanterns that were previously Coleman's brightest.

The NorthStar runs on Coleman fuel or unleaded gasoline. It features a patented push-button, electronic-ignition system powered by a AAA battery. An easy-to-attach tubular mantle avoids the strings of traditional mantles, and it burns brighter. The base of the NorthStar has a skid-resistant surface. Large control knobs make turning on and off, adjusting light output, and filling with fuel easier than ever. A permanently attached ball nut on the top of the lantern prevents loss of the nut and makes it easier than ever to take the lantern apart and put it back together.

The pump used to pressure the fuel doesn't need the twisting once required to lock and unlock a pump handle, and it is self-lubricating. It even includes a pressure indicator.

A globe guard protects the glass globe. The globe guard, globe, ventilator, and bail handle are removed all at once by loosening the ball nut, making it easier to replace the mantle.

The traditional Coleman lantern is a tough act to follow. More than 50 million have been sold since 1914, when company founder W.C. Coleman introduced his Arc Lantern.

Coleman's new Event Center is a storage container, dining table, and work surface in one. It is a 40½-in. collapsible, leafed table with a 37-quart stowage compartment in the middle. Its two leaves and integrated legs fold down for easy carriage, and it has a detachable padded shoulder strap. Two models are available, one insulated ($34) and one non-insulated ($29).

Coleman coolers have been camping standards for decades. In addition to hard-sided coolers, the company offers three collections of insulated cooler

(courtesy The Coleman Company)

(courtesy The Coleman Company)

Coleman PowerChill TE cooler

packs. The Adventure Collection, with eight models, includes fanny pack, backpack, and shoulder and bike style bags. The Bayside Collection is designed with the hiker and backpacker in mind; they're made of 150-denier ramie-polyester with Coleman logo zippers, pull tabs, and key clips, and are made to be used with Coleman Brite-Ice substitutes.

At the other end of the cooler spectrum are Coleman's new 40-quart PowerChill 12-volt thermoelectric coolers that stand upright and function much like refrigerators. The PowerChill TE ($99)

Coleman PolyLite jugs

(courtesy The Coleman Company)

than the Original; and the PowerLounger ($61), which functions both as a chair and as a sleeping pad.

The Crazy Creek ThermaLounger ($43) is a shell that fits over Cascade Designs' Therma-A-Rest self-inflating pads to produce a mattress/chair combination. The covers are made of 200-denier-coated packcloth. The ThermaLounger is available in regular, long ($51), Camp ($73), and Mini models ($36).

Kelty makes it easier to camp with children. Its new Kelty K.I.D.S. carrier system ($85–$165) makes a hike with kids enjoyable, not just bearable. All of the kid carriers in the system have automatic kickstands, no-pinch hinges, reflective tape, and the ability to accept sun and rain hoods.

The carriers are all made with 420-denier packcloth, high-impact buckles, and strong nylon webbing. They're designed to carry kids from about 6 months old to when they reach 45 pounds in weight. All the carriers accept accessory bags and pockets including diaper pack, diaper bag, sun or rain hood, and side pocket sets.

Okaman offers the BackSeat, a backpack and comfortable seat in one, which it calls perfect for camping, backpacking, canoeing, bird watching, and other outdoor activities. It offers up to 2,000 cubic inches of storage, with padded waist and shoulder straps. Quick-release buckles allow instant removal, and the tubular-steel pack frame converts into a comfortable seat. An optional snap-on backrest, stored in the pack, provides additional comfort. The BackSeat is available in an earthtone color and several camouflage patterns, in saddle cloth, fleece, or poly–cotton.

Peak 1, a Coleman brand, has introduced a new line of high-performance, butane–propane blended fuel appliances, including two lanterns: the Micro and the Electronic Ignition. The Micro Lantern ($31) stands just 7.2 inches tall and is attached to a 100-gram fuel cartridge. It produces light levels similar to a 75-watt bulb. The Electronic Ignition Lantern ($50) produces a light equivalent to about 80 watts from an electric bulb. It weighs 19.5 ounces with a small fuel cartridge.

can be used to keep food warm or cold and is powered by a cord that plugs into a standard 12-volt cigarette lighter outlet. It features a door that can be reversed for right- or left-hand opening. A smaller version, the 16-quart Personal Thermoelectric cooler is designed for day trips and short getaways.

To keep drinks cool, there's Coleman's new line of PolyLite jugs, with side-grasp flip spouts on all models, including ½-gallon and 1-gallon models.

Crazy Creek Chairs and ThermaLoungers are always camp favorites.

The Original Crazy Creek Chair ($44) is made from rugged 400-denier-coated packcloth, with ½-inch closed-cell foam and carbon-fiber stays. The chair is firm but flexible, provides comfort on any terrain, protects the sitter from wet ground, cold, and snow, and is lightweight and easy to carry. It even comes in a Large Chair ($49), which is 2 inches wider than the original.

Crazy Creek also offers the Long Back Chair ($52), 2 inches wider and 4 inches longer in back

Journal Entry: Family Camping & Blueberry Picking a Perfect Fit

Grandma would grasp a few berries in her crooked fingers, or carefully slide a plastic fork under a wedge of pie, and you'd see her eyes focus farther off, 25 years and 100 miles away, to an open patch in a northern forest.

Grandma never said much while picking wild blueberries in the flat wastelands of northern Lower Michigan, a short drive from our favorite family camping spot. She bent low, folding nearly in half at the waist. That shielded her hands, picking bucket, and mouth from the eyes of others. We kids figured she was the fastest picker of all. Only years later would Mom and Dad laugh and tell us they figured that one blueberry went into Grandma's mouth for each one that landed in the bucket.

By then Grandma was in a nursing home, and we were smuggling her little bags of wild blueberries, and maybe a piece of warm blueberry pie, on fresh summer days. The nurses pretended not to notice. For a little while, at least, we'd all be back in that blueberry patch not far from camp.

That's the power of a blueberry. It's a sweet fruit, widely distributed, free for the picking. It's also somehow part of a state of mind. Smart campers plan an outing that coincides with blueberry patches and the picking season.

I head for a berry patch soon after arriving at a favorite campsite each late summer. I'm seldom alone there, even if there's no human competition for the berries. Among animals that savor blueberries are water birds such as herring gulls, shorebirds such as cranes, gamebirds such as grouse and turkeys, and a long and noisy list of songbirds. Bears, foxes, opossums, rabbits, deer, and elk gather for a berry-patch feast, and chipmunks and mice scamper on the forest or bog floor.

Many people refer to *huckleberries* when they mean *wild blueberries*. The huckleberry is a seedier cousin. Blueberries grow in all the states from the Mississippi River eastward, and in California, Oregon, and Washington. Even parts of Idaho, Montana, Colorado, Nebraska, Oklahoma, and Arizona bear blue fruit. Top states, though, are New York, Pennsylvania, Michigan, Wisconsin, Minnesota, and those in New England states.

When to pick? The first berries are often munched in late June, and July Fourth is a good time to start checking out berry patches, especially in the southern parts of their range. A northern patch I camp near ripens in mid-August, and different blueberry species ripen in turn right up to the first frost.

Blueberries, says one text, "follow the ax and fire in forest lands." They're opportunists, one of the most resilient and among the first to move in after timber cover has been disturbed. Fire or logging can create a berry bonanza in just a couple of years, and the patch may remain generous for a decade.

Wild surroundings are part of the lure of wild blueberries. Be ready for them. Begin with clothing that covers your body to protect it from biting bugs, briars, and harsh sunlight. Stout hiking shoes, long pants—tucked into socks if you're in tick country—and long-sleeved shirt, along with a wide-brimmed hat, protect all but your face and hands. Use insect repellent (Chapter 9) and carry more in case you sweat away the first application. Take along plenty of water to replace that lost to perspiration. Use sunscreen to protect your face and neck.

Make sure you can find your way back when the picking's done, too. A map and compass (Chapter 15), and the know-how to use them, can make the path simple when you finally straighten up, full bucket in hand, ready to head back to camp.

How to begin a berry search? A good starting point is a forestry office. Find where fires or logging have created openings in the last few years. Another good bet? Ask a ranger at your campground where the berries grow. He or she has probably seen many family groups head out, bucket in hand, several generations mixing blueberries into their camping plans.

Many campers list a berry pail among their standard equipment.

Sources

All-Luminum Products
10981 Decatur Road
Philadelphia, PA 19154–3297
(215) 632–2800
Fax: (215) 824–1172

American Camper
Nelson/Weather-Rite
P.O. Box 14488
Lenexa, KS 66285–4488
(913) 492–3200
Fax: (913) 492–8749

Browning
One Browning Place
Morgan, UT 84050–9326
(801) 876–2711
Fax: (801) 876–3331

Buck Knives, Inc.
P.O. Box 1267
El Cajon, CA 92022
(800) 215–2825

Cabela's
Department 9BA–50M
Sidney, NE 69160
(800) 331–3454

Cascade Designs
4000 First Avenue South
Seattle, WA 98134
(800) 531–9531
E-mail: www.cascadedesigns.com

The Coleman Co.
P.O. Box 2931
Wichita, KS 67201
(800) 835–3278

Crazy Creek Products
P.O. Box 1050
1401 South Broadway
Red Lodge, MT 59068
(800) 331–0304
Fax: (406) 446–1411

Kelty, Inc.
113-B Industrial Drive
New Haven, MO 63068
(800) 423–2320
E-mail: supertioga@aol.com
Web site: www.kelty.com

Okaman Outdoor Products
101 First Street North, P.O. Box 239
Elysian, MN 56028
(800) 950–4296
Fax: (507) 267–4446

Peak 1
P.O. Box 2931
Wichita, KS 67201
(800) 835–3278

Chapter 5
Camp Clothing

Specialized clothing can make camping more comfortable. Sure, the things in your dresser and closet will work, but special fabrics, designs, clothing, boots, and rain wear will help you make the most of the terrain, climate, and weather that awaits you in camp. Never have campers enjoyed a wider or better selection of waterproof/breathable fabrics and membranes, insulation materials, and foot wear. What follows is just a sample of what's available.

Clothing provides more than comfort and fashion. It's the first line in defense against injury, insect attack, and sun dangers. See details in Chapter 9, "What's Bugging You?"

Gore-Tex: A Revolution in Waterproof/Breathable Wear

You don't buy Gore-Tex clothing, but you might well buy clothing with Gore-Tex within it: clothing made by W.L. Gore & Associates' manufacturing partners. You'll be more comfortable if you do. The clothing you select may feature Gore-Tex or another Gore membrane in one or more of several applications. The Gore membranes offer different kinds of weather protection and comfort.

Gore manufactures four types of membranes, each offering a mix of characteristics you can match

to the outdoor conditions you'll encounter. The characteristics are breathability, water protection, and wind protection. Which is most important depends on the climate, weather, and your activity level.

All the Gore brands are totally windproof. Of them, only Gore-Tex is totally waterproof. Waterproof means no water from outside can get in. Breathable means your body's natural moisture vapor can pass through the clothing to evaporate in the outside air.

Gore-Tex is very breathable, totally waterproof, and totally windproof. That makes it perfect for rain, snow, cold, and wind. Its durability is another plus. Gore-Tex is made of two substances. One is a membrane containing 9 billion pores per square inch, each much smaller than a droplet of liquid water but much larger than a molecule of water vapor. Liquid water is blocked, water vapor can pass, and the material itself doesn't absorb any moisture. The membrane is incorporated in one or more of several techniques.

Two-layer Gore-Tex Fabric includes a high performance fabric with the Gore-Tex membrane bonded to it. The result is supple lightweight weather protection.

Three-layer Gore-Tex Fabric consists of a high performance fabric with the Gore-Tex membrane bonded to it, and a knit liner fabric bonded to the other side. Designed for ultimate durability, it is often used to strengthen critical wear areas in garments using mainly two-layer construction.

In Gore-Tex LTD, the Gore-Tex membrane is bonded to the fabric used as the garment's lining. That puts the Gore-Tex very close to the skin, which is best for moving moisture vapor away from it.

Gore-Tex Z-Liners are hung between the outer shell and lining of the garment, resulting in a fully seam-sealed garment.

Gore's WindStopper membrane is very breathable and totally windproof, but doesn't offer any water protection. It's great for activity in cool or cold and windy conditions. WindStopper fabric is made by laminating Gore's WindStopper membrane to a high-performance fabric. It's especially effective in crafting windproof fleece for outerwear, gloves, hats, and other items. In cold and windy weather, it makes them more than twice as warm as ordinary fleece and just as breathable.

Gore DryLoft is extremely breathable, totally windproof, and water-resistant. Especially popular in sleeping bags and cold-weather parkas, it keeps insulation dry from the inside and avoids moisture build-up from light rain and snow or from condensation of perspiration vapor.

Gore's Activent is called the most breathable water-resistant, windproof fabric developed for outdoor activities.

3M Thinsulate Insulation

3M has been making Thinsulate insulation for seventeen years, and campers and other outdoor enthusiasts have come to rely on it; 90 percent of Thinsulate-insulated clothing buyers surveyed said they'd buy items with Thinsulate again, an extremely high degree of brand loyalty.

Insulation works by trapping air among fibers. The more air trapped, the better the insulation. Thinsulate fibers are smaller than 10 microns in diameter, one-tenth the size of a human hair. Thinsulate's tiny fibers allow more fibers in less space, trapping more air in less space than any other insu-

lating product used in the apparel industry. It is 1 ½ times the warmth of down, and almost twice the warmth of other high-loft insulation when equal thicknesses are compared.

Thinsulate insulation comes in several types:
- Thinsulate Type C insulation uses the structure of natural down as a pattern.
- Thinsulate Type B insulation, which resists compression, is used in footwear.
- Thinsulate Lite Loft insulation, especially good for outerwear and sleeping bags, offers the most warmth for the least weight of any synthetic insulation.
- Thinsulate Ultra insulation has a medium-loft structure that makes it favored in many clothing styles.
- Newest in the Thinsulate line is Thinsulate Type R insulation, made from 50 percent recycled polyester fibers including 27 percent post-consumer waste. Thinsulate Type R otherwise resembles the original Type C insulation.

3M, aware that we judge its Thinsulate insulation by the products we wear, works closely with manufacturers and makes sure they use the insulation correctly. Clothing makers must submit samples of their lines each year, as well as allow random in-factory and retail merchandise audits.

Layered Look

You can adapt to any cold or wet day by dressing in layers. The concept is simple: use several layers of light clothing, with a windproof or waterproof outer shell. Make sure there is enough venting to carry your perspiration away where it can evaporate.

When selecting layers, keep these material principles in mind:
- Cotton, especially denim, is loosely woven and lets water and air through. Neither works to your advantage except in tropical

heat. "Cotton kills," many backcountry experts warn.

- Down stops wind and holds heat unless it gets wet, and then it performs poorly.
- Synthetic materials such as Polarguard, Thinsulate, and polypropylene provide good insulation and let perspiration pass.
- Outer shells come in several fabric types. Nylon taffeta, for example, lets perspiration pass, but doesn't block wind well. Nylon microfiber lets perspiration pass and blocks wind, plus it can be surface treated to keep water out. Urethane-coated nylon is inexpensive and totally waterproof, but doesn't let your perspiration pass through. Breathable-coated nylon, moderately expensive, includes materials such as Ultrex, HP Ripstop, and Helly-Tech. Gore-Tex membrane blocks wind and rain well, even though it doesn't pass perspiration quite as well as microfiber or hold water out as completely as urethane-coated nylon. Most consider this expensive material the best compromise between breathability and water- and wind-proofness.

Clothing Products/Services

Acorn Products has taken a proven product, Malden Mills Polartec fleece, and put in on our feet. It was first in the field, with its sandalSox introduced in 1992. The ACORNSox line has since expanded to include many specialty socks. In all, more than fifteen styles of slippers, socks, and boots are offered.

Acorn's Outdoor/Versa-Tek performance socks ($12–$15) were designed for hiking, camping, and other outdoor activities. The socks feature light-weight comfort and thermal protection, rapid drying time, good shape retention, and maximum absorption of moisture from the skin to allow it to breathe.

Outdoor Versa/Tek socks are made of Polartec 200 fleece. Polartec, according to Acorn, starts as

100 percent polyester fibers and, more than 30 technological steps later, becomes high-tech, high-performance socks by Acorn.

"There is no reason to wear wool sports socks again," wrote ACORN CEO David K. Quinn in a release from the company. "The application of Polartec to sports and outdoor socks is the first revolution in hosiery since nylon replaced silk in stockings in the late '40s."

The ACORNSox line also includes Ultra Therm, designs especially suited to snowshoeing, winter camping, hiking, forestry, and other cold-weather applications.

ACORNSox made with Polartec from Malden Mills

American Camper's line of rainwear includes a Foul Weather Rainsuit made of nylon twill with a nylon-taffeta lining. A Professional Rainsuit is made of 50-millimeter. PVC/polyester backed material. American Camper's Ultra Rainsuit is made of PVC-coated nylon. The company also offers a Nylon/PVC rainsuit.

Other offerings in American Camper's wide line of rainwear includes an Industrial Rainsuit, Commercial Rainsuit, Rubber Rainsuit, rain parkas, and children's two-piece rainsuit.

Browning offers a Reversible Stuff-Lite Goose Down Parka, Jacket, and Vest that combine goose down, nature's best insulation, with the latest in fabric technology. Company staff say the garments seem almost weightless, are extremely stuffable, and very versatile.

Browning's new Barometric Gore-Tex Rainwear features an outer shell of lightweight Stratus Cloth with Gore-Tex Z-liner for complete protection from water and wind.

Cabela's Guidewear WindStopper Fleece Jacket is designed and sized especially for women, with a W.L. Gore WindStopper fabric that is completely windproof. The zip-front jacket features plenty of pockets.

Packable Nylon Raingear from Cabela's stores easily in its own pocket, with built-in straps so it can be carried like a fanny pack. The rugged lightweight nylon shell is made waterproof with a polyurethane coating. Seams are heat-tape sealed, and a mesh lining keeps the wearer dryer. The parka features zippered pockets with storm flaps, a drawstring bottom hem, and visored hood. It is available in men's and women's sizes and in several colors.

Columbia Sportswear designs, manufactures, and markets outdoor apparel and footwear. It charged to the forefront of the outerwear industry in 1982 when it introduced its Interchange System, a unique three-in-one jacket system that helped outdoor fans adjust their outerwear to changing conditions. By 1989 it had become the nation's largest ski and outerwear manufacturer.

Columbia says we're becoming more sophisticated: "Average consumers—not just 'techies'—now actively seek performance features such as waterproof/breathable fabrics, mechanical venting, waterproof closures, and Radial Sleeves, knowing that these features make outerwear more effective and comfortable."

The company produces products to meet that level of customer sophistication.

Columbia offers multi-purpose rain- and activewear in both water-resistant Perfecta Cloth and HydroPlus, and in Diamond Rip fabric, the latter a texturized ripstop nylon with a water-resistant coating. These items are lightweight and pack

Columbia Sportswear

(courtesy Columbia Sportswear)

easily, making them camping favorites.

Columbia's Performance Rainwear includes lightweight, waterproof/breathable jackets and pants with features such as reinforced top shoulders, mesh lining with wicking finishes, mechanical venting, waterproof closures with rain gutters, and Radial Sleeves.

A new jacket is made of HydroPlus 3000, a nylon taffeta with heavy waterproof coating which provides economical but effective waterproof protection. Columbia also offers PVC rainwear.

DuPont SealSkinz' line of waterproof socks now includes the Over-The-Calf style ($33), which the company calls the first socks on the market to provide waterproof coverage up to the knee.

Like the entire SealSkinz product line, Over-The-Calf socks have a patented, three-layer construction that provides a waterproof system. The inner layer is made of DuPont CoolMax, the same material used in All-Season SealSkinz ($24), to wick moisture away from the foot and disperse it throughout the sock. Insulated SealSkinz ($31) have a layer of ThermaStat fabric.

SealSkinz' inner layer spreads moisture over a larger surface area, which allows it to escape more quickly and efficiently through the sock's middle layer, which is a vapor-permeable membrane. That membrane lets perspiration escape while keeping water out.

DuPont SealSkinz waterproof MVT socks

The outside layer is made of DuPont nylon fabric for abrasion resistance and added protection.

SealSkinz are seamless to add comfort and prevent blisters. A cuff made of nylon/Lycra spandex keeps them from sliding down or losing their shape.

Fenwick's Motion Rain Jacket ($199) and Pants ($109) are made of nylon-ripstop fabric combined with Entrant, which is 100 percent waterproof and breathable. Each garment is seam-sealed for greater rain protection, and Darlexx waterproof fabric at the waistband and cuffs keeps out wind and water. Fenwick also offers a Lightweight Rain Jacket ($89) and Pants ($49), which fold easily into a pouch for storage and take-along convenience. Fenwick Rain Hats ($33) come in Western and crusher styles.

Fieldline's new Waterproof/Breathable Fleece Gaiters are made from SympaTex waterproof polyester fleece, to offer complete protection against rain, mud, snow, thorns, brush, and insects.

The gaiters feature Fieldline's exclusive Quick-Zip, a heavy duty Delrin zipper that zips from the top down and snaps securely in place. That makes the gaiter easier to attach to boots. Each gaiter fea-

tures a front-boot lace hook and spur grommets on the sides for attaching instep cords. The gaiters are secured by a drawstring at the top and a heavy-duty elastic band at the bottom and ankle.

Filson has taken its popular wool vest pattern and introduced it in a 100 percent Cotton Moleskin fabric, a tightly woven material with a plush face. The Filson Moleskin Vest is made of 12-ounce-weight fabric, and features two upper utility pockets and handwarmer pockets.

The Filson Double Mackinaw Cruiser ($237) is made of 100 percent virgin wool in 24-ounce Mackinaw Cloth. The company notes that many outdoor users still prefer wool, a premium natural insulator that retains much of its warming ability when wet.

Ideal for cold-weather camping, the Double Mackinaw Cruiser has a one-piece cape sewn over the basic Mackinaw Cruiser for insulation and protection from rain and snow. Mackinaw Field Pants ($130) are made of the same material.

Filson also offers campers the Mackinaw Cruiser ($195), Mackinaw Wool Vest ($76), Jac-Shirt ($130), pants, and other clothing. The Filson Shelter Cloth Traveler Vest ($116) is made of Shelter Cloth, an 8-ounce fabric made of cotton yarns and treated with a durable, water-repellent and stain-

Filson's Double Mackinaw Cruiser

resistant finish. Filson Moleskin garments are made of a tightly woven cotton fabric named for its soft likeness to the skin of a mole; the line includes a vest ($76), shirt ($87), and pants ($137). Filson also offers a full line of hats and caps for wear in all seasons.

Filson's new Upland Hat is made of the company's Dry Finish Shelter Cloth for protection against wind and rain. The 100 percent cotton, two-ply yarn fabric is Dry-Finish treated with a durable water-repellent and stain-resistant finish. A fold-down cape can be partially pulled down to protect the ears or all the way down to protect the neck and face. A 2-inch bill with dark green Moleskin undervisor cuts glare.

MPI distributes the Granger's line of waterproofing products, including many of interest to the camper. Granger's makes cleaning and waterproofing products for everything from traditional leather, wool, and oiled cotton to modern synthetics such as Gore-Tex, SympaTex and other membranes, Omni-Tech, Ultrex, Entrant, Cordura, and other materials.

The North Face, which makes premium quality clothing for rigorous outdoor applications, has introduced Tekware, a line of synthetic-fiber clothing that it says out-performs cotton in every category. Tekware, the company says, is "100 percent not cotton" clothing made of high-tech synthetic fabrics, designed for climbing, trekking, and adventure travel, but practical, comfortable, and fashionable about town.

Fabrics used to create Tekware include DuPont's Supplex, CoolMax, and Cordura Plus. They make the clothing strong, lightweight, quick drying, and shrink- and fade-resistant, and much less likely to tear, abrade, unravel, rot, or mildew. Tekware's VaporWick finish moves moisture away from the body for dry comfort.

Men's Tekware items include a Timberline Vest ($98) made with warm, lightweight Blackcomb Fleece, and the Explorer Shirt ($68) made of soft, woven Sumatra cloth. The Robson Plaid Shirt Jacket ($128) has a printed velour face and shear-

ling back for superior insulation. The Zambezi River Pant ($75) is made for rafting, kayaking, and other water sports.

For women, the Base Camp Shirt ($85) is made of a thermally efficient lightweight heather fleece. The Robson Plaid Shirt Jacket is made of Polartec Series 200 BiPolar Fleece with a water-repellent face and shearling back. The Ventilation ($72) and Sierra Madre ($48) shirts are perfect for excursions to places where staying cool is critical. Either teams well with the Tibetan Hiking Pant ($79).

Woolrich, at 166 years the oldest apparel maker in continuous operation in the U.S., offers a full line of outdoor sportswear and outerwear for men and women.

Women's styles feature softer finishes and more supple weaves for easy going comfort. A recent fall collection included the product categories Shirtings & Vests, Pants & Shorts, Skirts & Jumpers, and Sweaters.

Active outdoor men and women can choose Woolrich Teton outerwear: parkas, jackets, and the new Woolrich Matrix System of three-in-one, integrated component outerwear made of high-tech fabrics and finishes.

Men's and women's outerwear include garments made of Polartec's new Boundary Series of

(courtesy Woolrich)

Woolrich Elkhorn Corduroy Shirt, Snowden Cotton Henley Sweater, Reed Button-Down Shirt, Woolrich Turtleneck

Highlander Wool Jacket, Wool Baseball Hat, and Lewis Twill Pant

(courtesy Woolrich)

dense full-length fibers on both sides of the fabric for greater durability and higher loft. Of course, the company also features the fine wool garments on which its reputation was created.

Woolrich's men's woolen shirts include many updated styles with special weaves, including heavier weights and jackshirt styling. The company also boasts a large line of rugged, activity-ready sweaters.

Boots: Many Campers Go Feet First

Backpackers must pay particular attention to their footgear, because their feet are their primary vehicles through the wilderness. All campers, though, count on proper footwear to carry them on their adventures.

Day hikers on smooth, short trails can easily get by with tennis shoes, according to an expert backpacking friend. For overnight backpack trips, tennis shoes might suffice, but lightweight backpacking boots are better. Midweight hiking boots are the rule for extended backpack trips.

Industry Standards

Hiking boots come in several categories,

according to bootmaker Merrell Company.
- Trail shoes are low-cut hiking boots—half running shoe, half hiking boot.
- Day-hike boots are made for casual walks, scrambling on rocks, and mountain bike riding.
- Hiking boots blend moderate weight with maximum possible function. They're made rugged enough for multi-day outings; light enough for day hikes.
- Backpacking boots are made for long and hard hikes, carrying heavy loads. They're pricey but designed not to break down when tested severely in the backcountry.

With each step from trail shoes through backpack boots, the stiffness of the boot increases and, often, its price.

Get Fit

When fitting a boot for backpacking and other camping applications, insist on:
- a snug-fitting heel to keep your foot from moving within the boot, resulting in blisters or other discomfort;
- a snug instep fit for top balance and control; and
- room in the toe area; you'll be wearing heavy socks, and you don't want to jam your toes into the end of the boot when walking downhill. The staff of some specialty shops even test the fit by having you stand on an inclined plane, facing downhill, to simulate a slope.

Boot Products/Services

Browning Lady Ridge Top leather boots are extra tough and durable for rugged, mountainous terrain. Other new Browning boots include the Tundra and Pursuit Trail-Tech series of lightweight, all-leather hiking boots, and the new Nomad series of boots made with advanced construction techniques in advanced materials.

Cabela's new Black Mountain Hiking Boot ($79) is designed for serious hiking, with full-grain waterproof leather, sealed seams for additional waterproofing, and a polyurethane footbed and midsole to absorb shock. It also includes a Cambrelle-covered arch support that can be removed at day's end to let the inside of the boot dry.

Columbia footwear focuses on a concept it calls "cross-terraining," activities ranging from rocky slope scrambling to city street strolling. The Cold Creek line is geared for rugged walking. It includes three styles for men and women: high boot, low boot, and heavy-duty walking sandal.

Cold Creek footwear features waterproof full-grain leather, lightweight and durable Cyber-Lite midsoles, carbon rubber lug outsoles with steel shanks, and molded footbeds.

Dunham Bootmakers' new Dakota is a waterproof, insulated sport-utility boot, part of the company's "Great Footwear for the Great Outdoors" line. It features a direct inject, Dual Density Glacier sole system featuring two densities of polyurethane, and a full-grain leather upper. The waterproof leather is backed up by a breathable Gore-Tex bootie and Cambrelle liner, insulated with 600-gram Thinsulate thermal insulation.

Dunham's Montana 1000 features an Advanced Fastening System borrowed from the world of high-tech hiking boots. Its cinch roller system provides quick, easy, secure boot fastening.

(courtesy Dunham Bootmakers)

Dunham Bootmakers women's boots—Amy (left), Bow in leather (middle), and Bow in leather/Cordura (right)

The boot features a Gore-Tex bootie, and 1,000 grams of Thinsulate insulation, which company personnel say is the most available in outdoor footwear.

Dunham also offers three high-performance boot styles for women, including a range of linings, insoles, sole materials, treads, and construction features. Two styles of the popular Bow pattern feature Gore-Tex, and all three women's models are insulated with Thinsulate.

Merrell's Hiking line of boots, designed for long-weekend camping trips and quick day hikes, feature the company's exclusive waterproof technology, combining an Aqua Shield Liner with waterproof, non-wicking components. Leather uppers are treated with silicone and Scotchguard during tanning to produce a waterproof breathable leather.

Other features of Merrell Hiking boots include a gusseted, full-bellows tongue to keep dirt out; an instep stabilizer strap, dual-density footbed, and a new Vibram Foura sole.

Many bootmakers cement uppers to soles, Merrell says, but it still stitches them together in its Wilderness, a boot for the traditionalist.

Merrell's new Millenium Series of hiking boots combine the lightweight performance of trail running shoes with the traction and support of hiking boots. They feature waterproof reverse leather, said to be exceptionally abrasion-resistant, polyurethane foot frame, and rubber-toe bumper.

Merrell's Dayhiking boots offer uppers of leather and 1,000-denier DuPont Cordura, insole of recycled Texon, and contact sole of reground materials. Quick-dry linings move sweat and moisture away from the feet to keep them dry and comfortable.

Merrell Gore Tex (GTX) boots are tested in 3 inches of water for more than 500,000 flexes to make sure they meet the company's standards for guaranteed waterproofing.

Red Wing Shoes' Irish Setter boot line includes a new 6-inch boot, model No. 835 ($169) constructed of full-grain waterproof Birchwood Voyager leather, with a BQ–400 Thinsulate liner and waterproof Gore-Tex bootie. The boot has a Cordura upper, fully padded gusset with leather overlay, and removable Cambrelle-covered urethane footbed. A new Aurora pattern SuperSole has lugs on the forepart for traction, a larger surface area for greater wearability, and areas to release water and dirt.

For women, Red Wing offers the Red Wing No. 1603 chukka-height boot ($99), and No. 1604 full-height boot ($114) for work, hunting, or other outdoor pursuits. They feature full-grain Durango leather, and a Vibram Gumlite sole with a medium cleat lug for good traction.

Rocky Shoes & Boots has a new line of footwear that it says puts outdoor footwear on the streets. The Outback Series models feature all-leather and leather/Propox combinations.

The new boots are Gore-Tex lined to keep feet warm and dry. They're designed to be both rugged field boots and casual footwear. They come in a range of colors including brown, khaki, and three camouflage patterns, in 8-inch, 6-inch, and Oxford styles.

Rocky Tuff Terrainers, part of the Outback series, feature six styles of men's and women's boots in American-tanned waterproof leather with rust-proof eyelets, leather laces, and Rocky's Air-O-Magic air cushioned footbed. They come in 6-inch and Oxford styles, and most also feature a Gore-Tex bootie liner.

(courtesy Red Wing Shoe Company)

Irish Setter #835 6-inch boot

(courtesy Red Wing Shoe Company)

Red Wing women's style #1603

Sources

Acorn Products Co., Inc.
2 Cedar Street
P.O. Box 7780
Lewiston, ME 04243–7780
(800) US–ACORN

American Camper
Nelson/Weather–Rite
P.O. Box 14488
Lenexa, KS 66285–4488
(913) 492–3200
Fax: (913) 492–8749

Browning
One Browning Place
Morgan, UT 84050–9326
(801) 876–2711
Fax: (801) 876–3331

Cabela's
Department 9BA–50M
Sidney, NE 69160
(800) 331–3454

Columbia Sportswear
6600 North Baltimore
Portland, OR 97203
(503) 286–3676
Fax: (503) 289–6602

DuPont SealSkinz
1002 Industrial Road
Old Hickory, TN 37138–3693
(800) 868–2629

Dunham Bootmakers
P.O. Box 1289
Lewiston, ME 04243–1289
800-THE-BOOT, (800) 843–2668

Fenwick
5242 Argosy Ave.
Huntington Beach, CA 92649

Fieldline
1919 Vineburn Ave.
Los Angeles, CA 90032
(213) 226–0830
Fax: (213) 226–0831

C.C. Filson Company
P.O. Box 34020
Seattle, WA 98124–1020
(800) 299–1287

W.L. Gore & Associates, Inc.
100 Airport Road
P.O. Box 729
Elkton, MD 21922–0729
(800) 431–GORE

Merrell/Division of Karhu U.S.A., Inc.
P.O. Box 4249
Burlington, VT 05406
(800) 869–3348
E-mail: Wefit@karhu.ca
Web site: http://www.merrellboot.com

MPI Oudoors
85 Flagship Drive, Suite D
North Andover, MA 01845–6160
(800) 343–5827
Fax: (508) 685–2992
E-mail: outdoor1@ix.netcom.com
Web site: http://www.adventuresports.com/
asap/product/mpi/welcome.htm

Red Wing Shoe Company
314 Main Street
Red Wing, MN 55066–2337

Rocky Shoes & Boots, Inc.
13206 Carriage Road, Suite 202
Poway, CA 92064
(619) 486–3437
Fax: (619) 486–1850

The North Face
2013 Farallon Drive
San Leandro, CA 94577
(800) 447–2333

Chapter 6

On the Edge: Knives and Other Edged Tools

Knives are time-honored camping tools. Most of us don't use them often enough at home to stay sharp (pun intended) on their selection and maintenance. They vary from simple single-blade folding knives to multi-purpose tools that handle almost any camping task.

Blade Shapes

Knife blades come in several shapes, each with its own purpose, according to the personnel of Imperial Schrade Cutlery:

- Pen blades are good for light duty, including intricate woodworking and other precision tasks.
- Spey blades are used for tasks that require short, heavy-duty slicing.
- Clip blades are all-purpose blades used in many sporting and camping chores.
- Drop points are all-purpose blades that have more steel on the back and a lower point, allowing precise finger-tip control
- Skinning blades are designed for near-surgical accuracy in any skinning task.
- Shaped like a sheep's foot, a sheepsfoot blade is good for woodworking, farm chores, nonhammered chisel finishing, and work in tight areas where precision point control is required.

Handle Samples

Knife handles are made of many materials. Schrade offers a rundown of those most commonly used:

- Delrin and Staglon differ only in their appearance; they are durable, resistant to chipping, swelling, and breaking.
- Zytel is a space-age material, and handles of it are favored by outdoors enthusiasts who must limit weight but can't compromise on performance and durability.
- Resin-impregnated wood offers the natural beauty of wood with added moisture resistance and durability.

Maintaining Your Edge

Selecting a knife or other edged tool is only part of the camping equation. Restoring its sharpness is another one. Traditional camping wisdom teaches that a dull knife is more dangerous than a sharp one, because it's easier to make a bad move when forcing a faulty blade.

Fortunately for campers, tools are available that make knife sharpening, once a rare art, a breeze. Modern materials, and innovative sharpening systems such as GATCO's and Lansky's that take the guesswork out of blade angles, remove any

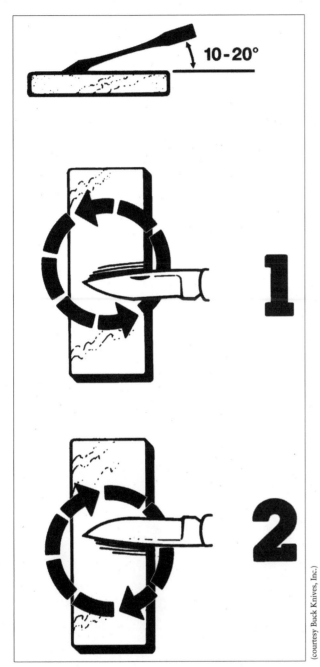

Steps for sharpening a knife on a stone

(courtesy Buck Knives, Inc.)

themselves in the stone. To sharpen the knife:

Sharp Ideas

1. Establish the correct angle and keep it. The ideal angle is 10 to 20 degrees, as shown in the diagram. The closer you stay to this angle, the better the edge you will achieve.
2. Use an even, circular stroke and slight pressure. It's best if your blade never leaves the stone. Make several full rotations in a counter-clockwise direction first, and count the number.
3. Turn the blade over and repeat the process, making the same number of smooth, circular motions in a clockwise direction. Repeat the paired action until you have the edge you want.

Products/Services

American Camper offers a stainless steel knife with multiple tools including 1½-inch and 2¼-inch blades, Phillips and flat-head screwdrivers, saw, scissors, leather punch, corkscrew, bottle opener, can opener, nail file, and awl.

The American Camper Key Chain Multi-Purpose Tool folds to fit in the pocket. It includes needle nose pliers, regular pliers, wire cutters, can and bottle openers, large and small screwdrivers, file, fish scaler, hook remover, and key ring. A Utility Tool features a nylon sheath and several handy built-in tools.

Camp scissors from American Camper include a knife, magnet, scissors, scaler, wire cutter, nut cracker, and other tools.

Browning knife blades are all made of 440C-type stainless steel, with precision fit and handles of genuine stag, quince, and other exotic materials. Signature Lockbacks have frames made of lightweight Zytel; two of them offer one-handed operation and can be switched from right-hand to left-hand design.

Browning Featherweight Composite Lockbacks have Zytel frames with laminated wood inserts.

excuse for using dull knives.

Many campers still sharpen blades on a sharpening stone, and that requires just three simple steps, according to the experts at Buck Knives, Inc.

Buck suggests using its Buck Honing Oil, and not ordinary lubricating oil, because the special honing oil will keep fine grains of steel from embedding

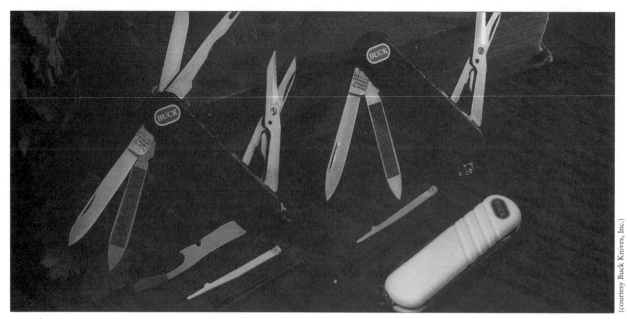

(courtesy Buck Knives, Inc.)

SwissBuck knives

Featherweight Composite Pocket Knives offer choices of clip, pen, and sheepsfoot blades, and scissors. Traditional pocket knives have genuine rosewood scales.

Browning's Folding Game and Camp Saw is a lightweight, durable saw with off-set teeth for rapid cutting.

Buck Knives is the best known, most respected, and most asked-for name in knives, according to company personnel. The firm traces its history back to Hoyt Buck's turn-of-the-century efforts to make steel hold an edge.

The Buck line includes fixed-blade sheath knives, pocket knives, folding lockblades, fishing knives, specialty knives, collectibles, Swiss-style knives, and hand tools.

The best-selling Buck is still the Model 110 Folding Hunter, introduced in 1963.

Buck's SwissBuck knives include fifteen models that offer combinations of handy tools and blades. They're made under a manufacturing/marketing agreement between Buck and Wenger of Switzerland, makers of Genuine Swiss Army Knives.

Buck Knives' Bucklite family of lightweight and rugged folding lockblade knives has been redesigned. All have a drop-point blade with bead-

(Courtesy W.R. Case & Sons Cutlery Company)

Case Pocket Worn knife

blast finish. Handles are high-tech engineering thermoplastic.

Other Buck knives of interest to campers include the Protege lightweight folding lockback knife, and the Crosslock series of eight knives that open one-handed.

Case offers a variety of cutting tools of use to campers. W.R. Case & Sons Cutlery Co. is a classic knifemaker whose tools have been sought by collectors, campers, and other users for decades.

Every Case blade is honed by hand, and made either of chrome vanadium or Case Tru-Sharp surgical stainless steel. Handles are made of genuine stag, genuine cattle bone, natural hardwoods, genuine mother-of-pearl, polished leather, or high-impact synthetics. Each knife is covered by a limited lifetime warranty.

Especially handy for campers are Case's XX-Changer knives, which offer four Tru-Sharp exchangeable blades: a clip blade for general outdoor use, drop-point blade for skinning game, fillet/boner blade for cleaning fish and game, and a saw blade with screwdriver tip for cutting wood or bone.

Campers who don't like new-looking gear can look for Case's Pocket Worn line of knives ($39–$59): new knives designed to look like they've spent years in a pocket. Special hand-finishing gives them a slightly smoother feel, with more rounded corners and cover rivets that are flush with the handle.

Each Pocket Worn knife features classic old red bone handles and high-polish blades made of Tru-

(courtesy The Great American Tool Company, Inc.)

GATCO *Double Diamond Pocket Hone*

Sharp surgical stainless steel. The line includes: Canoe, with spear and pen blades; Peanut, with clip and pen blades; Trapper, with clip and spey blades; Mini Trapper, with clip and spey blades; Stockman, with sheepfoot, spey, and clip blades; Small Pen Knife, with clip and pen blades; and Congress, with

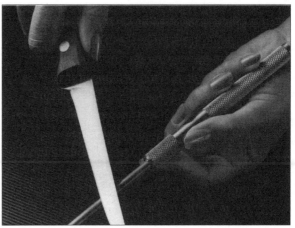

(courtesy The Great American Tool Company, Inc.)

GATCO *Diamond Stix Sharpener*

sheepfoot and spear blades.

Case has several sharpening accessories in its line, including a Diamond XX Sharpening Stone, Hard Arkansas Pocket Stone, Washita Arkansas Oilstone, plus oilstones, honing oil, ceramic sharpening sticks, pocket steels, and honing kits.

GATCO, the Great American Tool Company, sets the sharpening standard with its Knife Sharpening System, a clamp/angle guide that forces the knife sharpener to do what is otherwise nearly impossible: keep the blade at the ideal angle for the type of blade that it is. A thin fillet knife, for example, needs a narrower cutting edge than does a rancher's pocketknife or hunter's husky folding knife. Simply match the angle to the type of knife, and use holes in the clamp to move the sharpening stones at that angle across the blade.

GATCO Sharpening Systems feature custom molded cases with instructions permanently mounted inside; sharpening hones that are the industry's largest (5 by ¾ inches); integral sliding guide rods in the hones; stone holder with safety rails to protect the user's hands; honing oil; and of course, the knife clamp/angle guide that forms the basis of the system.

Systems are available ranging from a single-stone system, to the three-stone Edgemate, to the five-stone Edgemate Professional. GATCO also offers its ultimate, the Diamond Hone Sharpening System.

GATSTIX Ceramic V Knife and Scissor Sharpeners maintain razor sharpness on cutlery, and the Micro-X Pocket Ceramic Sharpener quickly sharpens knives, fish hooks, darts, archery broadheads, and serrated edges.

For those who prefer sharpening with a hone, GATCO makes its Double Diamond Pocket Hones, made of fast-cutting monocrystalline diamonds in four grades from coarse to ultra fine, as well as its aluminum-handled Diamond Stix Sharpener.

GATCO's Ax & Garden Tool Hone is a hockey-puck-shaped stone made to quickly and cleanly restore a strong sharp edge on cutting tools.

Gerber Legendary Blades has many edged tools perfect for camping. Its L.S.T. (light, strong, tough) Series combines premium quality high-carbon stainless steel with durable light weight handles made of fiberglass-filled Zytel. They're available in blades from 2 to 2¾ inches long.

Gerber E-Z-Out knives feature removable stainless steel carry clips, one-handed use, and light weight. Gerber Gator Fillet Knives include models with flexible rubber handles, and black-handled PowerGrip design. Serrated and straight blades are available.

In its line of outdoor recreation knives Gerber includes a Bolt Action exchange series of knives that allows the user to switch blades to match the task. The Pro-Guide series of hunting knives offer blades made of 400-series stainless steel.

To keep blades sharp, Gerber offers a ceramic Knife Sharpener, ceramic Pocket Sharpener, and retractable diamond sharpener.

Gerber also offers multi-purpose tools, including the Multi-Plier Tool, with thirteen tools made of heavy-gauge stainless steel. A simple flick of the wrist locks plier jaws into position with the motion

Schrade's Cliphanger Knife accessory system

(courtesy Imperial Schrade)

of just one hand. It is available with blunt nose or needle nose pliers in a satin or blackened finish. A Multi-Plier Tool Kit includes a coupler that will accept standard ¼-inch hex bits, and its sheath holds a Multi-Plier Tool.

Gerber also offers a Camp Axe, Sport Axe, and Sport Saw. Hollow axe handles are made of Polymid Fiberglass to reduce weight and avoid breakage. Their high-carbon stainless steel heads are molded into the handle. The Sport Axe weighs just 1½ pounds. The Sport Saw cuts on the pull stroke for added safety.

Imperial Schrade handmade knives boast features such as top-quality steel blades including its Schrade+ stainless steel, a special composition designed for superior edge holding ability, and stain- and rust-resistance. Schrade knives also feature solid nickel silver bolsters, solid brass liners, solid pin construction, unbreakable Delrin handles, and 100 percent hand-finished edges.

Among dozens of cutlery offerings from Schrade are the Old Timer, Uncle Henry, Outback,

Schrade Cliphanger, Lightweight Lockback, Extreme Survival, Schrade Scrimshaw, Imperial Apex Wilderness, Century, Tradesman, Jackmaster, and Diamond Edge brands.

The Schrade Extreme Survival knife features a forged 7-inch stainless steel blade. One edge is fine for cutting, while the top offers a file and saw rugged enough to cut metal, PVC, and wood. The blade also features a wire stripper, and the butt end features a stainless steel hammer and claw. The Extreme Survival knife was designed in cooperation with law enforcement agencies, but Schrade's staff say it's also suited to backcountry wilderness visits.

If your camping trip will include fishing, Schrade's Old Timer Maximum Flex and Minimum Flex fillet knives let you select the blade stiffness you like for cleaning fish for dinner. Each has a 6-inch-long Schrade+ Stainless Steel blade; soft, molded thermoplastic grip; and a rugged, ballistic-cloth sheath.

The Schrade Cliphanger series knives ($29–$36) clip onto a zipper pull or other loop, from which they can be quickly removed by a detachable clip. The easy-open, easy-close knives have Zytel handles and blades available in dual purpose—partially smooth, partially serrated—or full-serrated stainless steel designs.

Kershaw's line of quality knives includes its Blade Trader series.

The new Kershaw Cook's Blade Trader ($49) has blades to cover kitchen tasks such as slicing, dicing, cutting, carving, and paring. It features all-purpose, carving, and paring blades. All Blade Trader knives come in Cordura sheaths.

Kershaw's EdgeTek Blade Sharpener ($29) features superheated metallic carbides fused onto a bi-radial rod. The sharpener, which works with straight blades, serrated blades, saws, and other cutting tools, breaks down for storage in a webbed belt scabbard.

Lansky Sharpening Systems let anyone sharpen any knife, even one that's been abused. Each system comes in a colorful, lightweight, impact-resistant molded-plastic carrying case. Systems vary with the number and types of sharpening stones included. A system kit consists of a patented knife clamp with four angle guide holes; color-coded, slip-resistant finger-grooved hone holders with stones; special sharpening oil; extra screws; and instructions.

The clamp and honing stone guide establishes an exact stone-to-knife angle with each pass of the stone—30, 25, 20, or 17 degrees—depending on the hole selected.

Lansky also offers the Fold-A-Vee, a portable pocketable unit that restores cutting edges to knives, fish hooks, archery broadheads, and scissors. From its handy folded shape it opens in seconds and offers two preset angles of 17 and 25 degrees. The 17-degree edge is for sharp thin edges, while the 25-degree angle is recommended for knives that need a more durable edge.

The Lansky Sportsman Pocket Sharpener has two pre-set sharpening angles, 17 and 25 degrees, with high-alumina medium-ceramic sharpening rods that nest in their own hardwood storage base.

(courtesy Leatherman Tool Group)

Leatherman Super Tool

Lansky has also introduced a serrated edge sharpener.

Best known for its knife sharpening tools, Lansky also makes a strong space-age plastic knife with a serrated edge on one side and a beveled edge on the other. It features a cross-hatched, non-slip handle, and ridged thumb rest for a secure grip.

Leatherman Tool Group traces its history to Tim Leatherman's return from a low-budget trip across Europe that convinced him there was need for a compact knife that came complete with full-size pliers. Eight years later the company was formed, first producing the original Leatherman Tool, also known as the Pocket Survival Tool, then the Mini-Tool, which was introduced three years later.

Leatherman's Super Tool includes full-strength pliers, two knife blades, a wood/bone saw, four screwdrivers, and many other useful tools in a compact design, which includes a locking system for blades and tools in use.

The new PST II is based on the full-size, full-strength pliers of the original Pocket Survival Tool, but with improvements including strong and useful scissors.

Leatherman's newest tool is the Micra, half the size of any other Leatherman product, and based on spring-action scissors instead of needle-nose pliers. It weighs 1.75 ounces and measures 2.5 inches long when closed. Besides scissors, the Micra includes tweezers, flat and Phillips head screw-

drivers, bottle opener, clip point knife, nail file/cleaner, ruler, and lanyard attachment.

McGowan Manufacturing's FireStone Knife Sharpener is designed for safe, easy sharpening of knives ranging from pocket to hunting knives, and kitchen to utility knives. FireStone sharpeners feature a comfortable handle grip made from recycled plastic jugs. A built-in guard separates the hand

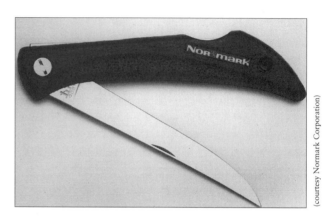

Normark Folding/Camping Fillet Knife

from the sharpening area for safety. Free rotating stones are made of abrasives in a base of industrial porcelain, providing a clean, new sharpening surface with every blade stroke.

The FireStone Knife Sharpener is available in a single stage model, or a two-stage model for a more refined, polished, and longer-lasting edge.

The FireStone Fillet Knife & Hook Sharpener comes in two models, each with FireStones for easy mistake-free sharpening.

Normark Corporation offers a line of Rapala fixed-blade hunting and camping knives, blending contemporary design and old-world craftsmanship. They're made by Marttiini of Finland, which makes the popular Rapala Fish'N Fillet knife. Five knives in the new line are designed to meet the needs of hunters and campers.

The Rapala Soft-Grip Hunter/Camper is an all-around knife, with Rapala Soft-Grip handle. It can be used for varied activities, company staff say, such as cutting rope and slicing a steak. Other knives in the line are more specifically designed for

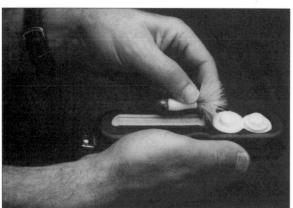

FireStone Knife & Hook Sharpener

hunting applications.

Normark has also introduced its Presentation Folding/Camping Fillet Knife, with a 5-inch-long Swedish surgical stainless steel blade, a black molded "Comfort Grip" handle, and a sturdy lock-back design.

Normark offers Tri-Hones, complete sharpening systems featuring three grades of stone: Arkansas Perfect/Washita, Arkansas Perfect/Hard, and Arkansas Perfect/Abrasive. The stones are mounted on a triangular centerpiece that rotates on a wooden base. Rotate to the surface you want. The Tri-Hone unit comes in three sizes.

Normark also offers Arkansas Perfect Hard Stone-on-sticks, with a hard Arkansas novaculite in stick form, available on either a wooden handle or base.

Normark sharpening kits offer paired whetstones and honing oil. Individual stones are also available, and the Perfect Angle Knife Sharpener has preset guides, a four-sided sharpening rod, and three grades of Arkansas Perfect Whetstones, plus a hook hone.

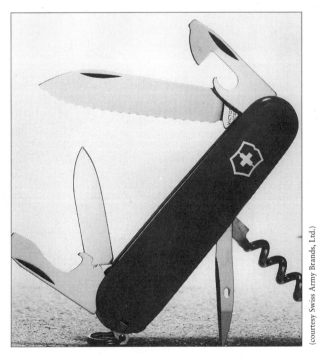

Victorinox Swiss Army Knife Weekender

(courtesy Swiss Army Brands, Ltd.)

Remington has a complete line of fixed and folding knives. All Remington knives carry lifetime warrantees for the original purchaser. Each knife features blades of 440A stainless steel or carbon steel, and handles of either Delrin stag, resin-impregnated hardwood, or slip-resistant Kraton.

Grizzly Series lockback knives are made of 440A stainless steel with Kraton handles, featuring the Remington logo. Several blade options and configurations are available. The 9500 Series includes folding knives with blades of easy-to-sharpen carbon steel, brass liners, and nickel-silver bolsters. They range from 2¾ inches to 4¼ inches long when closed.

Remington also offers its traditional folding pocket knives with blades of 440A stainless steel, brass liners, and nickel-silver bolsters. Other Remington offerings include Stren-brand fillet knives, made with stainless steel blades and Kraton handles.

Victorinox Swiss Army Brands is known for its knives of many features.

The new Victorinox Weekender ($31) can be used as an all-purpose camping utensil. It features a large serrated locking blade that can slice food. The Weekender's other features include a small blade, can opener with small screwdriver, bottle opener with large screwdriver, wire stripper, tweezers, and toothpick.

A novel new Swiss Army Knife is the Illuminator ($30), featuring a range of useful implements including a bright red, LED mini-light built into its 2¼-inch case. Simply press the Victorinox cross-and-shield logo, and the red beam of light illuminates dark corners of tents and backpacks. It uses LED technology instead of short-lived bulbs, so Victorinox personnel say the knife should provide 10,000 hours of light.

The Illuminator features many Original Swiss Army Knife implements, including a small blade, scissors, nail file with screwdriver tip, and toothpick. Another model ($33) features a steel chain and ring that makes it handy to hold keys or to attach it to camping gear.

Sources

American Camper
Nelson/Weather–Rite
P.O. Box 14488
Lenexa, KS 66285–4488
(913) 492–3200
Fax: (913) 492–8749

Browning
One Browning Place
Morgan, UT 84050–9326
(801) 876–2711
Fax: (801) 876–3331

Buck Knives, Inc.
P.O. Box 1267
El Cajon, CA 92022
(800) 215–2825

W.R. Case & Sons Cutlery Co.
Owens Way
Bradford, PA 16701
(800) 523–6350

GATCO
The Great American Tool Company
P.O. Box 600
Getzville, NY 14068–0600
(800) LIV–SHARP
Fax: (716) 877–2591

Imperial Schrade
7 Schrade Court
Ellenville, NY 12428–0981
(800) 2–SCHRADE

Lansky Sharpeners
P.O. Box 800
Buffalo, NY 14231–0800
(716) 877–7511
Fax: (716) 877–6955

Leatherman Tool Group
P.O. Box 20595
Portland, OR 97294
Web site: http://www.leatherman.com

McGowan Manufacturing
25 Michigan Street
Hutchinson, MN 55350
(800) 342–4810
Fax: (612) 587–7966

Normark Corporation
10395 Yellow Circle Drive
Minnetonka, MN 55343
(612) 933–7060
Fax: (612) 933–0046

Remington Arms Company, Inc.
870 Remington Dr.
Madison, NC 27025
(800) 243–9700

Victorinox
Swiss Army Brands Ltd.
One Research Drive
Shelton, CT 06484–0874
(800) 243–4032

Chapter 7
Recreational Vehicles

*R*ecreation vehicle (RV): (1) a vehicle that combines transportation and temporary living quarters for travel, recreation, and camping; (2) a fun way to camp.

RVs include folding camping trailers, conventional travel trailers, fifth-wheel travel trailers, truck campers, van conversions, and mini and full-size motorhomes. RVs range from simple places to sneak a nap, to luxuriously appointed lodges on wheels.

One American household in ten owns a recreation vehicle, found a survey by the University of Michigan's Survey Research Center, and one in four is interested in buying one in the future.

The average age of an RV owner is 48. Younger RVers are more likely to own folding camping trailers or truck campers; more mature RV owners are more often found camping in motorhomes, conversion vehicles, travel trailers, and fifth-wheel trailers.

The biggest argument in favor of an RV? It's a feeling all campers treasure: being able to go where and when you please.

There are currently 9 million RVs on the road, according to the Recreation Vehicle Industry Association (RVIA), with 100,000 new families buying RVs each year. RV owners travel an average of 5,900 miles and spend more than twenty-three days on the road each year.

Money Talks

RV travel can be a cost saver, too, according to a vacation cost comparison study conducted by PKF Consulting, for the Go Camping America Committee, a promotional industry group.

A family can get 50 to 80 percent more vacation for its money when traveling and camping in an RV, the report found. The consulting firm studied twelve different vacation formats, including five in which travel, lodging, and most meals took place in an RV the family already owned.

RV camping vacations cost about half as much as driving the family car and staying in hotels, 60 percent less than traveling by bus or train and staying in a hotel or motel, and 70 percent less than flying to a vacation destination and staying in a hotel.

"The findings of this study show that RV vacation savings are so significant," said Gary LaBella of the RVIA, "that it wouldn't take many trips to recover the initial cost of the RV."

An RV Run Through

Which RVs are which, and how much do they cost? RVIA is a good source for information, and provides these guidelines and estimates:

There are two kinds of RVs: those you tow or carry on your vehicle, and those you drive. Tow-

Before You Go

By KOA

Some of the most important vacation planning steps you'll ever take have nothing to do with destinations, maps, or reservations. These are the critical steps you take to prepare for your holiday and take the "traps" out of your camping trip.

Before you leave:

- Have your vehicle checked by a mechanic to ensure fluid levels are up, belts and hoses are in good condition, tires are in good condition and properly inflated, and other systems are in tip-top shape.
- If you're towing a travel trailer or fifth-wheel, make sure everything inside the unit is operating correctly, inspect the tires and bearings, double-check that all components of your trailer hitch are properly secured and in good condition (both on your tow vehicle and on your trailer), and verify that your indicator lights and brake connections are working correctly.
- If you travel in a motorhome and tow a car or other vehicle, make sure that your tow dolly is in good shape and that the indicator light connections— and brakes, if you have them—are functioning correctly.
- Leave a key with a neighbor or trusted friend who can check your home on a regular basis, care for pets, remove flyers from your door knob or steps, and so on. Leave this person a number where you can be reached, or an alternative means to get in touch with you, if necessary.
- Make arrangements for all deliveries—mail, newspapers, etc.—to be held until your return. If these items consistently sit on your porch for hours until someone comes to pick them up, it's obvious that you've gone on vacation.
- Buy electronic timers, and use them to set lamps and a radio to go on and off at various times throughout the day to give the illusion that someone's home.
- Arrange to have yard work done on a regular basis while you're gone. If your usually neat yard becomes a jungle, it tells potential burglars that your home is empty and an easy target.

With these steps out of the way, you're free to plan a worry-free vacation.

able RVs include folding camping trailers, truck campers, and travel trailers. Motorized RVs include motorhomes and conversion vehicles such as vans.

- *Folding camping trailer:* A lightweight unit, its sides collapse for easy towing, even behind rather small cars. Set up, it provides space for cooking, dining, and sleeping for up to eight people. Prices range from $2,000 to $10,000, with an

average of $4,453. Sales of these handy vehicles rose 20 percent in one recent year alone.

Truck camper sales are currently at their highest levels in two decades.

- *Truck camper:* Classified with the towable rigs, this camping unit is loaded onto, or affixed to, the bed or chassis of a pickup truck. Many have kitchen and bathroom facilities. They can sleep two to six people.

Viking fold-down camping trailer

(courtesy Viking RV)

Ultra Light Travel Trailer by Coachmen RV

(courtesy Coachmen RV)

Ranger Truck Camper by Coachmen RV

(courtesy Coachmen RV)

With prices ranging from $2,500 to $15,000, the average price is $9,803.

- *Travel trailer:* This unit is towed by a car, van, or pickup truck. Travel trailers offer comforts such as kitchen, bathroom, dining and living areas, electric and water systems, and modern appliances. They can be unhitched from the tow vehicle to make local travel convenient. Travel trailers can sleep from four to eight people. The average sale price is $12,034, but prices can range from $4,500 to $53,000.

- *Fifth-wheel trailers:* These are travel trailers designed to be towed by pickup trucks with special hitches. Their special raised forward ends extend over the bed of a

pickup. Average price is $19,420.

Among motorized RVs are:

- *Motorhome:* This camping and travel vehicle is built on, or as part of, a motorized vehicle chassis. Kitchen, sleeping, bathroom, and dining areas can be reached from the driver's area. A motorhome usually offers electricity, heating, air conditioning, water, and propane gas systems. Available in sizes from mini to extra-large, motorhomes can sleep from two to ten people.

- A compact Type C mini motorhome, built on a conventional van frame, costs an average of $37,193; a larger Type A model, built on a specially designed chassis, might cost $67,216. A top-of-the-line rig can carry a tag of more than $100,000.

- *Conversion vehicles:* These are vans, trucks, and sport-utility vehicles made by their original manufacturers, then modified in appearance for transportation and recreation by a company specializing in that service. Changes might include side windows, carpeting, paneling, custom seats, sofas, and other accessories. Most popular are van conversions, which can seat from seven to twelve and sleep two to four. They sell for an average of $25,492, and range from $15,000 to $41,000.

Maverick Class C mini-motorhome by Georgie Boy

(courtesy Georgie Boy Manufacturing)

Coachmen Van Camper

(courtesy Coachmen Vans)

Rent an RV

Unsure which kind of RV best suits you? Simply want to enjoy the RV lifestyle without buying and maintaining your own? Consider renting a unit from one of the more than 400 rental outlets nationwide. RV rentals have grown by about 30 percent each year since 1986, according to the RVIA. The largest company, Cruise America RV Depot, has more than one hundred rental outlets in the U.S. and Canada.

While all kinds of RVs are available for rent, motorhomes account for 90 percent of the business. Depending on the season, deluxe motorhomes rent from $70 to $170 per day, which is just the cost of a hotel or motel room at many destinations. Truck campers and travel trailers average $50 to

$120 per day.

RVIA staff says your Yellow Pages' "Recreation Vehicles—Renting and Leasing" heading will carry local options. For nationwide RV information, check out "Who's Who in RV Rentals" ($5) or "Rental Ventures," ($3), a 28-page full-color guide to renting an RV in North America. They're available from the Recreation Vehicle Rental Association.

Whether you're driving a motorhome, conversion vehicle, or other tow vehicle, make every trip a safe one by buckling up your safety belt and making sure passengers are secured too. Wearing a safety belt is the single most effective thing you can do to prevent serious injury and death in a traffic accident, according to the National Safety Belt Coalition.

A guide to RV safety, produced cooperatively by RVIA and the American Association of Retired Persons (AARP) is available by writing RVIA, Department AARP, P.O. Box 2999, Reston, VA 22090; include $1.25 for postage. The guide includes basic instructions and tips that are useful to all drivers, no matter what their age or driving experience.

RV Financing: Flexible

Financing a RV purchase is easy, with attractive interest rates and flexible payment plans, and often with tax advantages, says RVIA.

Lenders, first of all, like RV buyers. They make their payments.

Loans for new large RVs generally range from ten to twelve years, with some stretched out to fifteen years. Most lenders require less than 20 percent down, others up to 30 percent. Loan terms for used RVs usually call for 20 to 25 percent down payments, and payback periods of four to eight years.

For most RV buyers, interest on their loan is deductible as second-home mortgage interest. To qualify, the RV must be used as security for the loan, and must have basic sleeping, toilet, and cooking accommodations. Most RVs fit that description. The Internal Revenue Service (IRS) publishes two booklets containing helpful informa-

Driving an RV is Different, not Difficult

By RVIA

Driving or towing a recreation vehicle (RV) opens up a world of on-the-road travel adventure. It requires no special license and it's easier than many newcomers think.

A survey of RV owners by Louis Harris and Associates found that three out of four RV owners did not feel that driving or towing an RV poses any difficulty. In fact, experienced automobile drivers already have the skills to drive a motorized RV. Automatic transmissions, power brakes, and power steering are practically standard equipment.

With proper attention to the differences in vehicle size, height, and weight, you'll find it fun and easy to take the wheel of a conversion van or motorhome. Towing skills are also readily acquired.

Whether you will be driving a motorized RV or towing an RV, you should:

- Adjust and use all rear view mirrors. Before leaving on a trip, sit in the driver's seat and adjust all mirrors for optimal road views.
- Account for your vehicle's width and length when turning. The front and rear wheels will track paths much farther apart than those of a car.
- Allow more time to brake, change lanes, and enter a busy highway because bigger vehicles take more time to accelerate and slow down.

Drivers towing a folding camping trailer or travel trailer should also:

- Match the proper tow vehicle to your RV. Most full and mid-size family cars can pull a trailer, and so can today's popular vans, 4x4s, and light-duty trucks. Check the owner's manual to find the trailer types that your vehicle can haul and the maximum load weight it can pull.
- Use the right trailer hitch and make sure it is hitched correctly.
- Connect brakes and signal lights. Always check that the trailer's brakes, turn signals, and tail lights are synchronized with the towing vehicle's.
- Back up with care. If you place your hand at the bottom of the steering wheel, the trailer will move in the direction of your hand. To move the trailer to the right, move your hand to the right. Once the trailer is moving in the proper direction, avoid any sharp movements of the steering wheel. Slowly steer the vehicle into its desired direction. It is also a good idea to have someone outside the vehicle help the driver back up to avoid any obstacles not seen in the mirrors. If another person is not available, the driver should inspect the area behind the vehicle. By evaluating the situation before backing, drivers can avoid surprises and accidents.

tion. *Publication 936—Home Interest Deduction* and *Publication 523—Selling Your Home* are available by calling the IRS at (800) 829–3676.

RV Living: Not Roughing It

Some people figure camping means roughing it. RV owners know better.

Many new private campgrounds are designed especially for RVs, and luxury RV resorts often offer a menu of features such as tennis courts, golf courses, and even health spas.

Also available are RV package trips, caravans to destinations where entertainment and activities are arranged for you. One company offering these trips, Woodall's Trails-a-Way, said in a recent release that its business continues to climb, with the most popular destinations being Alaska, national parks, and country music magnets Nashville, Tennessee; Branson, Missouri; and Myrtle Beach, South Carolina.

At Season's End

RVIA, in its pamphlet, *Wintertime RV Use and Maintenance,* ($2) offers these coldweather storage tips:

- Drain all water tanks, lines, and pumps to prevent damage to the RV's water system;
- Use non-toxic RV anti-freeze to keep any remaining water from freezing the system;
- Run the engine of a motorhome at least one half-hour each month, or drive the motorhome at highway speed once a month for at least 10 miles, to keep it in good working order during extended storage periods.

Sources/Products

Coachmen Industries makes all five kinds of recreation vehicles, from folding tent trailers to deluxe motorhomes. It recently realized a milestone—its 500,000th recreational vehicle—when a 1996 Leprechaun mini-motorhome rolled off the line. The company that was to become Coachmen was first formed in 1964, when the first Coachmen Cadet travel trailer was manufactured.

Coachmen Clipper and Sport folding camping trailers offer easy, comfortable camping. The Clipper comes in five sizes; the economical Sport in two. Both Clipper and Sport models offer color-coordinated fabrics, side curtains, high-density 4-inch-thick cushions, bed-end curtains, home-style countertop, stainless steel sink, liquid propane range, built-in icebox, and other features.

Coachmen's Ranger pickup camper is available in five floor plans and lengths from 10 to 11½ feet. It features power-operated stands, shower, electronic ignition furnace, three-burner range, and queen-size over-the-cab bed. With an available twin bed arrangement, it can sleep up to five people.

Coachmen's new Ultra Lite travel trailers are light enough to be towed by minivans, light pickup trucks, and utility vehicles. Innovations include a large front-end storage compartment, aerodynamic front profile, and drop-down bunk. The trailers are 17 feet 8 inches, and 19 feet 11 inches long, and both less than 3,000 pounds The longer trailer features a shower and two-basin kitchen sink, and can be ordered with optional bunk beds.

Catalina travel trailers are available in a dozen models from 26 to 36 feet long, and most offer slide-outs to boost living space. The Catalinas sleep from four to nine people, depending upon the model.

Coachmen's Royal fifth wheels and travel trailers are designed to offer convenient travel with all the style of hotels and resorts but with far fewer hassles. Four Royal fifth-wheel trailers are available in models ranging from 30 to 36 feet, 10 inches long. Each includes a hydraulic slide room that conveniently increases the living area. Royal travel trailers come in 30-foot 5 inch and 32-foot 5-inch models. Royal fifth-wheel and travel trailers offer front and rear fiberglass caps, deluxe exterior graphics, fiberglass insulation, and a rubber roof among their features.

Coachmen Maxxum fifth wheels come standard with a slide-out room. The trailers are available in lengths from 30 to 39 feet and sleep four to six people.

Coachmen offers several lines of motorhomes, including the Catalina line of Class C mini-motorhomes, which is available in models ranging from 20 to 29 feet long. The motorhomes feature roller shades, radius slider windows, jackknife sofa, side dinette, and reclining pilot and passenger seats. Galleys include three-burner range top, lighted range hood, double-door refrigerator, and stainless steel sink.

The Coachmen Destiny motorhome has been updated with many new stylish features. Its new Mirada Class A motorhome is designed to be affordable, with four models available on Ford or Chevrolet chassis.

Coachmen's Santara Class A motorhome has been redesigned to offer even more luxury and convenience, including stylish new front and rear caps and a new grill. Its huge windshield offers greater visibility. Bus-type basement compartments offer handy storage. Some models even offer a rear back-up camera option.

The Coachmen Leprechaun mini-motorhome, first introduced 26 years ago, continues to evolve with camper-pleasing features such as new floor plans, large view-grabbing windows, and stain-resistant carpets.

Coachmen Vans is a separate entity within Coachmen Industries. The Saratoga blends the elegant features of a conversion van with the practical and economical benefits of a motorhome. Built on a 19-foot-long. Dodge chassis, it features a kitchen with refrigerator, dinette, two-burner stove, and microwave. It also offers sleeping accommodations for two in twin sofas that easily convert to a queen-size bed.

Coachmen Van Campers are built on General Motors, Ford, or Dodge 19-foot-long chassis, with swivel passenger seats, comfortable sleeping accommodations, and functional kitchens. Some models offer an overhead bunk. Rear bathrooms feature a shower, marine toilet, clothes hamper, and wardrobe. Standard features include three-way refrigerator, two-burner stove, microwave, electronic-ignition water heater, propane furnace, and holding tanks.

Coleman Folding Trailers by Fleetwood include the Grand Tour Series, with six models. The large Niagara features a hydraulic lift system and shower/cassette toilet. The Yukon offers dining area seating and a 26-cubic-foot front storage trunk accessible from both outside and inside.

Coleman Destiny trailers include the Bayport, with large wrap-around dining area and two queen beds. The Cheyenne has a large front storage trunk. The lightweight Laredo weighs in at less than 1,000 pounds.

Standard features of Coleman trailers include one-piece seamless ABS roofs with Luran S. Sunbrella 302 acrylic tenting offering high breathability to let humidity and cooking odors escape, and it won't rot or mildew.

Georgie Boy, the third largest maker of Class A motorhomes, is now a Coachmen Industries company. It retains its own management and identity, with brand names including Cruise Master, Cruise Air, Swinger, Encounter, and Pursuit.

Georgie Boy's new Maverick mini-motorhomes come in 23- to 30-foot-long models with a one-piece rear cap, laminated exterior, easy to maintain interior, and plenty of storage space. They are available on Chevrolet or Ford chassis.

Jayco manufactures camping trailers, travel trailers, fifth wheels, mini-motorhomes, truck campers, and van conversions. Jayco's Eagle Series is a functional, economical line of camping trailers, led by the new 8 ST with its front storage trunk. Eagles range in campsite length from 17 feet 4 inches to 24 feet. Ten- and 12-foot U-shape lounge models offer comfortable sleeping for seven adults. Other models sleep six. Jayco's exclusive, smooth-operating and patented lifter system is fully enclosed and protected from the elements.

The Jayco Jay Series is America's most popular selling camping trailer, claim company personnel,

with campsite lengths of 21 feet 6 inches and 24 feet. The Jayco Jay can accommodate six or seven adults, depending on the floor plan. New Boltaflex CT tent fabric is rugged synthetic fabric combining style and durability. Windows are tinted for privacy, heat reduction, and protection from ultraviolet rays. Interiors offer features such as ice box, oak-framed cabinetry, and functional galleys. Some models offer options such as outside shower, bath-shower package, or overhead cabinetry.

Eagle travel trailers and fifth wheels by Jayco combine plenty of attractive features with economy-minded pricing. New on Eagles is a power drive rack and pinion slide-out system for dinettes. Fifth wheels have increased interior headroom and a straight roof line for improved aerodynamics.

Jayco's Eagle SL travel trailers and fifth wheels have aluminum-frame lightweight superstructures that make them easier to tow behind lighter fuel-efficient vehicles. Seven Eagle SL trailers range from 21 to 24 feet long; three fifth wheels range from 22 to 24 feet long.

Jayco's Designer Series towables—travel trailers and fifth wheels—offer luxury features at a mid-line price, says company staff. Exterior features include radius corners, and smooth molded fiberglass end caps. Inside are designer-coordinated interiors with high-line fabrics and carpeting, and custom-crafted oak cabinetry.

The Jayco Sportster fold-down truck campers

come in five models, from 7 feet to 9½ feet long. All but one have full-height entrance doors, and are designed to fit full-size and short-bed trucks. A patented roof-lifter system and easy-tuck canvas tent combine for an easy-to-erect home-on-the-road.

Eagle Series mini motorhomes by Jayco come in six models that range in length from 21 to 29 feet. Models include three wide-bodies with "basement" storage. Eagles feature an aluminum frame, brighter interior lights, and contemporary decor. They're available on Ford or Chevy chassis.

Jayco's Designer mini motorhomes are built for the discriminating traveler, with rich appointments in models from 22 to 29 feet long. Three wide-body units combine plentiful living space with

(courtesy Jayco)

Jayco Jay Series camping trailer

(courtesy RVIA)

Kids inside folding tent camper

(courtesy Coachmen RV)

Coachmen Leprechaun Class C mini-motorhome

"basement" storage. Interiors are a blend of oak and deluxe fabrics and carpets.

The Recreation Vehicle Industry Association represents nearly 500 RV manufacturers and component parts suppliers, who together produce about 95 percent of all RVs manufactured in the U.S.

RVIA is a clearinghouse for information on recreation vehicles. Among other publications it offers a *Catalog of Publications and Videos about the RV Lifestyle,* with descriptions and ordering information on publications such as *Recreational Vehicles: Finding the Best Buy,* by Bill Alderman, Jr. and Eleanore Wilson; *Rental Ventures,* by the RVIA; and *Living Aboard Your Recreational Vehicle,* by Gordon and Janet Groene.

For free information geared toward those new

Shasta 220 RK mini-motorhome

Shasta 30-foot travel trailer

Family exiting van conversion; youth looking through binocular.

to RVs ask for: *The Go Camping America Vacation Planner,* a free color guide to RV trip planning. It is available by calling (800) 47–SUNNY.

The *Camping Vacation Planner,* a 16-page publication of the Go Camping America Committee, is a glove box–size planner that includes phone and address listings for franchise and independent campgrounds and RV parks, national campground directories, RV dealer associations, RV rental com-

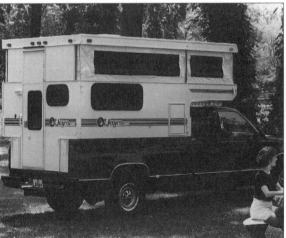

Jayco Sportster fold-down truck camper

Star Brite Rain View

Winnebago Minnie motorhome

panies, camping clubs, and camping enthusiast publications. It also contains helpful tips on preparing for your trip and setting up camp. For RV campers, there is advice on shopping for and choosing the right unit, as well as rental information. It is available by calling toll-free, (800) 47–SUNNY.

Shasta, a Coachmen Industries company, offers a full line of RVs, from lightweight travel trailers to mini-motorhomes.

Shasta's new Light Laminated Towable (LLT) is a compact, lightweight trailer built to appeal to both young families and veteran campers. It comes in 19 and 21 foot lengths, and is light enough to be towed by mini-vans, most sport-utility vehicles, and light trucks.

The Shasta 30-foot-long model 305DB offers double bedrooms: a spacious front master bedroom with storage underneath, and upper and lower bunks next to the roomy bathroom at the back of the unit. When combined with a dinette and jack-knife sofa, the trailer sleeps eight people.

Shasta's 225 Rear Kitchen fifth wheel offers a spacious rear kitchen, center living/dining area, large walk-through bath, and upper level walk-around queen bed or optional twin beds, which combine to sleep up to six people.

The Shasta Wide Body 220RK mini-motorhome is 23 feet 6 inches long, on a Ford chassis with a 460 cubic inch V-8 engine and 55-gallon fuel tank. It features tilt wheel, cruise control, emergency start switch, single arm swing-away mirrors, cab-over bed, private bathroom, and stylish fiberglass running boards.

Star Brite manufactures specialty products designed for care of recreation vehicles.

Star Brite Premium RV Polish with Teflon is the company's latest advance in RV polish/wax products. Wipe it on, let it dry, and wipe it off. No hard rubbing or buffing is required to obtain a deep shine with long-lasting protection and weather resistance. It works on fiberglass, metal, and painted surfaces. Ultraviolet inhibitors protect the surface from the sun's rays, and Teflon protects against weathering and repels stains, dirt, oil, road film, salt, and other surface spoilers.

Star Brite Liquid Electrical Tape protects RV electrical connections. The liquid vinyl seals out moisture and prevents corrosion on wires and terminal junctions. It's especially good for light connections, generator terminals, and other electrical

(courtesy Star Brite)

(courtesy Winnebago Industries)

connections exposed to the elements, says company staff.

For RV holding tanks and portable toilets, there's Star Brite Fresh Toilet Treatment 6 Paks, with a non-formaldehyde, environmentally safe formula to quickly and efficiently break down waste and control odor.

The RV view stays clear with Star Brite's Rain View, a blend of polymers that makes glass and most plastic surfaces so slick that wet weather slides off for improved visibility with and without the use of windshield wipers.

Viking fold-down camping trailers are available in several series and sizes, within the deluxe Legend and affordable Saga lines. Combined, they offer eleven floor plans in 12- to 16-foot-long models. Viking is a Coachmen Industries company.

Viking trailers feature air-conditioner-ready roofs, roof vents, high arched bunk bows, roller assisted beds, rustproof polypropylene wheel wells, portable in/out dining tables, laminated one-piece exterior aluminum skins, and one-piece floor.

Winnebago Industries traces is roots to the mid-1950s, and offers the Winnebago, Itasca, Vectra, Luxor, and Rialta brands of motorhomes. The company provides a wide range of models and floorplan options.

The Winnebago Minnie and Itasca Spirit motorhomes include models that range from 21 to 29 feet long. Several bedroom modules are offered in the 29-foot models as is a new double bed arrangement.

The Winnebago Minnie Winnie and Itasca Sundancer lines are wide-bodied, basement models that offer extra room. Both lines include a new 31-foot motorhome, with almost 25 percent more interior and exterior storage space than its predecessors.

The fuel-efficient, front-wheel-drive Rialta line has been expanded to include models with a full-size corner bed or twin beds.

Winnebago's Adventurer line has also been expanded; there are three new standard width models with slide-out extension systems to boost living space.

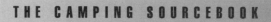

Sources

Coachmen Recreational Vehicle Company
P.O. Box 30
Middlebury, IN 46540
(219) 825–5821

Coachmen Vans
P.O. Box 50
Elkhart, IN 46515
(219) 262–3474

Coleman Folding Trailers by Fleetwood
P.O. Box 111
Somerset, PA 15501
(814) 443–7297
Fax: (814) 443–7340

Georgie Boy Manufacturing, Inc.
69950 M–62
Edwardsburg, MI 49112
(616) 663–3415

Jayco, Inc.
Box 460
Middlebury, IN 46540
(800) 785–2920

Recreation Vehicle Industry Association
P.O. Box 2999
1896 Preston White Drive
Reston, VA 22090–0999
(703) 620–6003
Fax: (703) 620–5071

Recreation Vehicle Rental Association
3930 University Drive
Fairfax, VA 22030
(800) 336–0355

Star Brite
4041 Southwest 47th Avenue
Ft. Lauderdale, FL 33314
(800) 327–8583

Viking Recreational Vehicles, Inc.
P.O. Box 549
Centreville, MI 49032
(616) 467–6321

Winnebago Industries, Inc.
P.O. Box 152
Forest City, IA 50436
(800) 643–4892
E-mail: 722.62.472@Compuserve.com

Chapter 8
Camp Cooking

For many of us, camping means camp cooking. Here we'll talk about simple cooking, but also about cast-iron cookery, portable ovens, and more. I baked my own 40th birthday cake, laced with fresh-picked wild blueberries, in a cast-iron Dutch oven in a campground. You can make special camp foods, too.

Dutch Oven Cooking

A Dutch oven is a portable cast-iron cooking pot. It comes in two forms: a footless pot with rounded top to be used on a range or in an indoors oven, and footed oven whose lid is flanged to hold coals or charcoal briquettes for outdoor cooking. The latter, obviously, is of most interest to the camper.

According to the experts at Lodge Manufacturing, a group called the International Dutch Oven Society formed about a dozen years ago, to share tips and teach newcomers how to get more out of their Dutch ovens. With about 1,500 members worldwide, the organization even holds annual Dutch oven cooking competitions.

Charcoal is a Charm

You can fire your Dutch oven with wood coals if you wish, but many specialists count on charcoal;

it is always accessible and produces more predictable temperatures.

Experts construct charts for their Dutch ovens, which tell the number of charcoal briquettes need-

This roast duck was prepared for the author's 40th birthday in a Dutch oven.

ed above and below an oven of a specific size to generate a desired level of heat within it. One chart, for example, prescribes twenty-five briquettes—seventeen on the top, eight below—on a 12-inch Dutch oven to generate a temperature of 350 degrees. Of course, as briquettes burn down they need to be replaced with fresh ones to maintain that heat.

Other experts aren't as scientific. One friend slides a few briquettes beneath his oven, piles up as many as will fit on the lid, and goes hunting for a couple of hours while a roast, with potatoes and carrots, cooks perfectly.

Like most cooking, expertise comes individually, through trial and error. Dutch ovens, happily, are very forgiving of errors and rich in their reward for success.

Backpacking Food

Backpacking provides a special challenge when it comes to food. You're burning up extra energy chugging down the trail and carrying all your equipment and food on your back. You need plenty of good chow, but you don't want to carry more weight than necessary.

One solution is to purchase food that is freeze-dried, which is cooked and then processed so all the water is removed from it. Hot water reconstitutes the food, and you have an instant meal from lightweight ingredients. The freeze-drying process and the packaging are costly, though. And while these specialty foods taste far better than those offered just a few years ago, they still usually pale next to the real thing.

Real Food?

The other option is to bite the bullet and lug "real food" along, trading the extra burden for the satisfaction of a meal like Mom used to cook.

Most of us split the difference by mixing a bit of efficiency and a bit of self-indulgence in our pack.

Some experts divide camping foods into several categories. Fresh foods are best tasting, of course,

but their moisture makes them heavy and spoilable. They're good choices for the first day or two. Canned foods remain unspoiled, but they're hefty, and they leave cans to lug back out. Low-moisture and dehydrated foods such as dried fruits, dried meats, and fruit leathers are lighter, keep well, and can be chewed as-is, or soaked or simmered to soften them. Dried foods such as powdered milk, dried beans, and pasta products, have been low-cost camping staples for decades. Some new food offerings are called "retort" foods, and they're high-moisture foods in durable foil pouches. They can be warmed by dropping them in boiling water for a few minutes, and then served right out of the container. Freeze-dried foods, previously discussed, include a wide range of items for which the camper trades a little taste and a fair amount of expense for the ultimate in lightness.

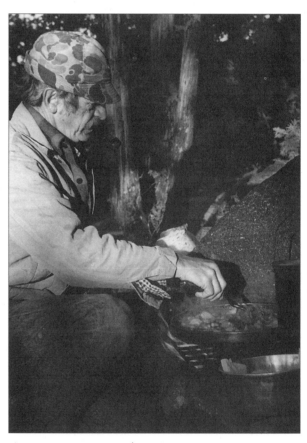

For many campers, it's not camp cooking if it's not done over a campfire.

An Evolving Menu

First-night backpack meals, for example, might well include steak, baked potato, and even a salad. The meat can be frozen at the start, and carried in a leak-proof container. Such an enjoyable meal is only a burden for the first few miles, when you're freshest, and really starts a long journey off on a festive note.

As additional backpacking days unfold, it becomes increasingly wise to use foods whose water has been removed. Commercial backpack foods are nearly trouble-free, although you're wise to try some first to see if you agree with the manufacturer's idea of what makes a meal for the listed number of people. Many hard-charging backpackers say a "meal for two" is just right for one hungry backpacker.

Seasoning Cast Iron

If you're lucky enough to own a veteran piece of cast iron cookware, you know how easy-to-clean it is. If you purchase a new item, you can take steps to prepare it for generations of good cooking.

According to the folks at Lodge Manufacturing, the largest producer of cast iron cookware in the United States, seasoning, the process through which pores in cast iron absorb oil and create a natural, non-stick finish, is simple.

Begin by washing, rinsing, and thoroughly drying the new cookware to remove its wax coating. Mild soapy water works best; never use abrasive detergents.

Next, put a tablespoon of solid vegetable shortening in the cookware. Warm the utensil to melt the shortening, then use a cloth or paper towel to coat the entire surface, inside and out, all corners, edges and lids.

Heat the cookware upside down at 350 degrees for one hour. Place aluminum foil or a cookie sheet beneath it to catch any drippings.

Remove the utensil from the oven, and wipe the cookware with a paper towel.

The skillet or Dutch oven is now ready for cooking.

Detergents can remove seasoning, so Lodge's Billie Hill suggests cleaning cast iron cookware with just hot water and a stiff brush. But even well seasoned pieces, says Hill, sometimes need reseasoning.

"Seasoning is a process," said Hill. "The more you use cast iron, the better it gets, but if your pan doesn't have a shiny finish, you should repeat the seasoning process."

Other important cast iron care tips include:
- Always wash the utensil with hot water, rinse it completely, and dry it thoroughly;
- Cook food with low-water content and low acidity the first few times you use a new piece of cast iron;
- Uncover hot food when you remove it from the heat source, because steam can remove the protective coating;
- Rust means the pan needs reseasoning;
- Cook at medium to medium-high temperatures; cast iron heats evenly, so you don't need to use extremely high cooking temperatures;
- Store cast iron utensils with tops or lids off, so moisture can't collect and cause rust; a paper towel placed inside the utensil will absorb any moisture.

You can also assemble your own lightweight backpack foods. Pasta, especially macaroni and spaghetti, are lightweight winners. Study recipe labels closely to make sure they don't call for things such as fresh milk or eggs that you're not likely to have along. You can cut corners, though, by adding powdered milk or eggs.

Other solid choices that need little care are salami, crackers, gorp (good old raisins and peanuts), and granola bars. Instant hot breakfast cereals are simple to fix, eat, and clean up. Pancake flour, biscuit mix, drink mixes, instant mashed potatoes, and dried soup mixes are other grocery store items that help you beat the high cost of camping equipment stores.

Our family likes both backpacking outings and traditional car-carried camping. We try some of the lightweight foods and methods while car-camping, to make sure they'll work in the backcountry, too. It's good practice and great fun.

Backpack Cooking

Backpackers are often barred from cooking on wood fires, either by rules or shortages of wood. Most count on small camp stoves to cook their chow.

Stoves are available that run on white gas, unleaded gas, kerosene, butane, propane, and even wood and wood fiber. Your choice will depend on personal preference and your budget.

Most popular are white gas stoves, and those that run on either white gas or unleaded regular gasoline. They generally weigh 2 to 3 pounds when full of fuel and will boil a quart of water in five to seven minutes.

Products/Services

Alco-Brite offers gelled ethanol products that can be used to cook, boil water, or keep warm.

Alco-Brite's Camp & Utility Stove is made of heavy-duty extruded aluminum and designed for use with the company's fuel canisters. Several other Snap-On Stove models are available. Cook n' Heat canisters come in 8- and 16-ounce sizes. A 16-ounce can burns up to 4½ hours, producing 2,500 British thermal units (BTU), enough to boil water in eight to ten minutes, or fry an egg in four to five minutes. Squeeze bottles of Alco-Brite Fire Starter are available in 4-, 16-, and 32-ounce packages.

American Camper offers everything you need for camp cooking, from propane stoves to plastic serving ware. The Low Profile Propane Stove is a single burner that generates up to 8,000 BTUs. A Deluxe Double Burner Propane Stove features full rear and side wind screens. Camp Matches, available in piezoelectric and refillable butane models, make lighting camping appliances a snap.

American Camper cooksets are available in cast iron, enameled steel, stainless steel, and aluminum. Many of the cooksets feature plates and cups in bright, easily cleanable plastic. The company also has a full line of accessories, including cooking forks, silverware sets, percolators, and cooking grills. A Folding Picnic Table offers a table top measuring 34 by 26 inches. Collapsible water carriers are available in 5- and 2½-gallon sizes. Smaller canteens, water bottles, and bota bags are also available.

Athena portable butane gas stoves from Aervo-Pacific Co. are compact and lightweight for easy carrying. The model 1U90 is three stoves in one; it can be used as a stove, grill, or wok. It weighs a little more than 8 pounds, and runs about two hours and ten minutes on an 8-ounce can of butane.

The Athena Pocket Stove fits in the palm of the hand and weighs just 1.2 pounds, yet generates more than 7,000 BTUs. It runs on isobutane fuel, available in 2- and 6-ounce cans. Piezoelectric ignition eliminates the need for matches.

Coleman's cooking stoves have been part of camping for generations—the Model 1 was introduced in 1923—and they continue to evolve. The company's big new Guide Series Three Burner Propane Stove is designed for cooking meals for a crowd. The design allows three full-size pots to sit side-by-side or a griddle to straddle two burners.

Coleman Electronic Ignition Gas Stove

Coleman Guide Series Three-Burner Propane Stove

(courtesy The Coleman Co.)

(courtesy Fox Hill Corporation)

Sportsman's Oven

Each burner lights independently, the main burner generates 15,000 BTUs while the other two generate 10,000 BTUs each. The cook top lifts out for cleaning.

Coleman has introduced four models of liquid fuel stoves with electronic ignition. Turn on the gas, click the electronic ignition knob a time or two and the main burner fires up. The same procedure works with the second burner. Electronic ignition is available in two dual-fuel stove models, and two Coleman-fuel-only models.

Camp cooking is made easier with Coleman's High Stand, a folding stable platform to lift camp stoves and chest coolers to handy working height. The new version is made of anodized aircraft aluminum

tubing. Accessory racks make the stand even handier.

Fox Hill has made it possible for campers to enjoy baked goods and meals in the bush or on the trail. Its Sportsman's Oven ($49) is made of heavy-gauge embossed, rust-resistant aluminum. The 2-pound, 11-ounce oven measures 10 by 10 by 6 inches, and uses one burner of a camp stove, propane stove, woodstove, gas or electric stove, single burner stove, or other heat source. An external dial thermometer keeps you updated on the baking temperature.

The Sportsman's Oven can handle biscuits, muffins, baked fish, meatloaf, baked potatoes, and other foods. It comes complete with a temperature gauge, non-stick baking pan, chrome baking rack, recipes, and instructions.

Fox Hill's larger Outfitter Oven ($59) is 10 by 10 by 9 inches and weighs 4 pounds 2 ounces. It comes with two 8- by 8- by 2-inch non-stick baking pans, chrome baking rack, side handles, and other features. The middle shelf of the Outfitter Oven can

Journal Entry: Backcountry Cooking

Camp cooking, to wilderness guide Gene Dessellier, is simple. "The most important thing," he said with a laugh, "is being able to eat whatever you cook."

Dessellier had just kept a party of seven well-fed for five days in Ontario's Quetico Provincial Park. Fare ranged from freeze-dried beef and noodles, to steaks, to fresh-baked bread, much cooked over wood fires.

That brand of good cooking in the backcountry—or at any camp—begins with good fire-tending. "The fire is very important," said Dessellier as he tended steaks on a wire rack over a wood fire contained by an impromptu rock fireplace. "You want the coals to get down to an even heat. The wood should be good, and here that's a little hard to find. Maple is excellent, and pine is terrible." One good firewood some people neglect is what Dessellier calls "beaver wood," aspen or birch from which the bark has been peeled by beavers. Bark on, the wood rots. But with the bark removed the wood usually dries hard and produces a hot cooking fire.

It's worth the fuss of finding wood. "I like to do all the cooking on wood," said Dessellier. "I much prefer it. For big groups, it's about the only way to cook enough food for everyone and serve it hot.

"And there's also the aesthetics," he added. "It just seems more like camping with a wood fire."

Freeze-dried and dehydrated foods are the backpacker's staples, but Dessellier said a mix of those instant foods and fresh foods makes for a more enjoyable camp. "You have to use the fresh stuff up in a day or two, depending upon what it is and the weather. But that's usually no problem," he said with a laugh.

"My favorite is steak," said the cook. "No, I like fish better, actually. Fish is indigenous" (this camp cook is a high school math teacher, and occasionally a big word slips out) "and there's a whole lot of it. It's a lot better than freeze-dried food," although those backpacking meals have improved in taste substantially over the past decade or so.

Camp breakfasts also lend themselves to "real" cooking; pancakes, bacon, eggs, and French toast are quick to fix and camp favorites.

Whatever the meal, Dessellier said that with a good supply of wood nearby, it can take as little as forty-five minutes after igniting kindling to be eating. More typically, though, figure on an hour or two. Of course, learning to graciously let time slip by is part of camping.

Outfitter Oven

(courtesy Fox Hill Corporation)

Lindy Grill-Pac

(courtesy Lindy-Little Joe)

cookware, including skillets, chicken fryers, griddles, bakeware, serving ware, and camping cookware, with the Dutch oven leading the line.

Dutch ovens come with rounded tops for indoor cooking, and flanged tops for outdoor cooking with wood fire embers or charcoal briquettes. The latter is of most interest to the camper, and Lodge obliges with standard models from an 8-inch diameter 2-quart oven to a 16-inch across 12-quart oven. There's even a baby 5-inch-diameter Camp Oven with a 1-pint capacity.

Skillets run the gamut from the 3-inch Miniature Skillet to a mammoth 20-inch model that weighs 21 pounds! Covers, square skillets, and specialty skillets are also in the line, along with specialty fish cookers and stew pots. Cast-iron griddles make cooking great campsite bacon, eggs, French toast, and pancakes a breeze.

MPI offers Esbit solid fuel tablets, and a line of tiny stoves powered by them. The tablets, which can be used for warmth or heating, generate 1,400 BTUs, and burn for 15 minutes per ½ ounce cube. One cube will bring a pint of water to a boil in less than eight minutes.

The Esbit Camp Stove measures 3 by 4 by ¾ inches and weighs 3¼ ounces. The fold-down stove has supporting side projections to improve and centrally focus the heat output. The Camp Star is a flat 4½- by 4½-inch steel star scored to be folded for personal safety or survival use and fueled with an Esbit solid fuel tablet. The Wing Stove is a reusable, fold-down three-legged metal stove with a center cup to hold Esbit fuel tablets.

Nature's Fire offers several 100-percent natural products for starting campfires and other fires, plus complete cooking fire products. There's nothing to break, explode, spontaneously combust, or cause chemical burns, and no litter is left behind.

Seventeen aromatic hardwoods and agricultural products are used in Nature's Fires' 25- and 45-minute Complete Cooking Fire packages, the latter enough to cook a full meal for up to six people.

be removed to provide more space for large items such as a beef roast, whole chicken, or loaf of bread.

Lindy-Little Joe's Grill-Pac is a cast-aluminum grill that features a 10- by 13½-inch surface. It packs down into an 8- by 10- by 2½-inch water-proof zippered case and weighs just 4¾ pounds. A unique anchor coil augers into the ground to hold the grill securely, and the grill can be adjusted up to 7 inches high, without tools, and swings away from the fire to add wood or move cooking gear.

Lodge Manufacturing is a 100-year-old family-owned company specializing in cast-iron cooking gear. The company produces a full line of cast-iron

(courtesy Peak 1)

Peak 1 Apex II Stove

Campfire Starter is designed to create a fire at an elevation of 6,000 feet at a temperature of -30 degrees Fahrenheit in a 30-mile-per-hour wind. Just one tray, company personnel say, will start the wettest wood on fire under the most adverse conditions.

Open Country is an extensive line of camp cookware and accessories from The Metal Ware Corp., and includes a Deluxe 6-person Camp Set with 10-, 4-, and 2-quart kettles with covers, 10-inch fry pan with non-stick interior, 5-cup camp percolator, six 8-inch plastic plates, six 8-ounce plastic cups, and steel handle.

Other Open County sets include a 6-Person Weekender Camp Set, 4-Person Deluxe Camp Set, and several Backpacker cook sets. A Backpackers Pack Grid can be used on wood or charcoal fires, and features a double outer rim to prevent snags within packs and to stop food from rolling off.

A special premium grade of camp cookware, the Alpine Series from Open Country is made of stainless steel, with copper-coated pan bottoms to heat quickly and evenly.

Open County also offers a selection of classic-style canteens and camping bottles, and several camp-style percolators including one that makes twenty cups of coffee at a time.

Peak 1, a Coleman division, has introduced a new line of high-performance, butane-propane blended fuel appliances, including five single-burner stoves and two sizes of 70/30 butane/propane fuel cartridges.

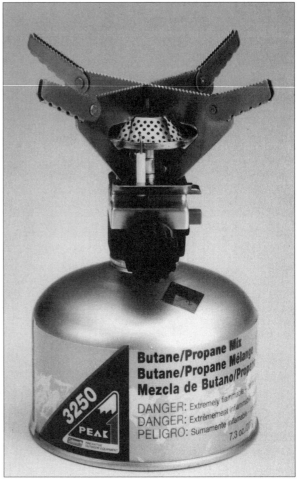

(courtesy Peak 1)

Peak 1 Backpack DLX Butane Stove

The stoves, like lanterns also included in the line, use generated fuel systems for fewer flare-ups, wide adjustability ranges, and precise flame control. The Micro Stove ($25) weighs just 5.6 ounces and fits in the palm of the hand. Attached to a full 100-gram Peak 1 fuel cartridge, it still weighs just 12.2 ounces, but produces 13,000 BTUs of heat. It boasts a three-minute eighteen-second boil time for a quart of water in a covered pot. On the hottest stove setting, it burns for twenty-four minutes on a small cartridge.

The Electronic Ignition Stove ($45) features matchless lighting, and produces 16,000 BTUs. It weighs just 10.3 ounces and boils a quart of water in two minutes forty-five seconds. Three other stoves in the line have power ratings of 12,000 to 14,000 BTUs.

Peak 1's high performance 70-percent butane/30-percent propane blend provides better starting and operation of appliances in cold weather and higher altitudes. Propane, which vaporizes at lower temperatures, gets burning better, quicker. The fuel blend comes in 100-gram ($3) and 227-gram ($3.80) cartridges, both with large-diameter bases for stability and resealable cartridges so the canister can be removed and used again.

Peak 1 also offers five liquid fuel stoves, including multi-fuel models and the highly acclaimed Apex II multi-fuel component stove.

Peak 1's Feather and Multi-Fuel single burner stoves have also become backpacking standards, along with liquid-fuel lanterns and propane stoves and lanterns. Peak 1 also offers a full line of stainless steel cookware. Pots feature either locking bail handles or swing-out wire handles. Several cooking kits are available to match the size of the camping party and its equipment weight and size requirements.

Pyramid calls its Oven Cooking Systems the most innovative and versatile anywhere. The pyramid shape focuses heat and creates a vertical draft. The stoves are made of durable high quality stainless steel.

Only nine charcoal briquettes are needed to cook enough food for as many as six people with the 12-inch Pyramid, company staff says. A patented Super Heat Grate allows charcoal to be placed in a vertical arrangement so each briquette reaches a higher temperature. By changing the configuration of briquettes you can bake, boil, fry, roast, smoke toast, grill, or steam your food, all with the same cooking stove. It can be fueled with charcoal bri-

quettes, wood chips, or Sterno.

The hinged design of the stoves lets them fold flat for easy carrying and storing. They set up in fifteen seconds, without tools.

Pyramid also makes the CampMaster Duo campstove/oven/grill, which uses the same principles of thermal feedback, plus a complete line of Pyramid accessories. The Pack-lite Plus stove for backpacking, hunting, fishing, and camping, burns charcoal or gas with an optional gas attachment. It weighs just 40 ounces.

Traveling Light, a Cascade Designs company, makes the Outback Oven, which allows the camper, even the backpacker, to bake anything—pizza, cake, casserole, or whatever—he or she can bake in an oven at home. Company personnel say it can turn a stove into a temperature-controlled oven, reduce fuel consumption on every meal by one-third, and provide cooking versatility.

All four Outback Oven models include an aluminized fiberglass convection dome, diffuser plate with riser bar, thermometer, reflector collar, mesh storage sack, and backcountry baking booklet. The models range from the 7-ounce Ultralight, to the 3-pound Outfitter, which comes complete with a 12-inch Teflon pan with nesting lid.

Traveling Lite also makes the Platypus line of collapsible water bottles. The bottles don't add a plastic taste to water, can be frozen or boiled, make a simple solar shower, and can even become a pillow or insulated cushion. They come in 1- and 2-liter sizes. Bottle accessories include jackets, holsters, fanny pack holders, and a reservoir system that includes a drinking tube.

Sources

Alco-Brite
P.O. Box 840926
Hildale, UT 84784
(801) 874–1025
Fax: (801) 874–1026

Athena
Aervoe-Pacific Company, Inc.
P.O. Box 485
Gardnerville, NV 89410
(800) 227–0196
Fax: (702) 782–4027

The Coleman Co., Inc.
P.O. Box 2931
Wichita, KS 67201
(800) 835–3278

Fox Hill Corporation
Department TCS
P.O. Box 259
Rozet, WY 82727
(800) 533–7883

Lindy-Little Joe
Box C, 1110 Wright Street
Brainerd, MN 56401
(218) 829–1714
Fax: (218) 829–5426

Lodge Manufacturing Co.
P.O. Box 380
South Pittsburg, TN 37380
(423) 837–7181
Fax: (423) 837–8279

MPI Outdoors
85 Flagship Drive, Suite D
North Andover, MA 01845–6160
(800) 343–5827
Fax: (508) 685–2992
E-mail: outdoor1@ix.netcom.com
Web site: http://www.adventuresports.com/
asap/product/mpi/welcome.htm

Nature's Fire, Inc.
P.O. Box 356
Ellsworth, MN 56129
(800) 491–3473
Fax: (507) 967–2383

Open Country
The Metal Ware Corporation
P.O. Box 237
Two Rivers, WI 54241
(414) 793–1368
Fax: (414) 793–1086

Peak 1
P.O. Box 2931
Wichita, KS 67201
(800) 835–3278

Pyromid
American Innovation Marketing
3292 South Highway 97
Redmond, OR 97756
(800) 824–4288

Traveling Light
Cascade Designs
4000 1st Ave. South
Seattle, WA 98134
(800) 531–9531
Web site: www.cascadedesigns.com

Chapter 9
What's Bugging You? Insects, Sun and Poisonous Plants

Certain concerns seem common to camping wherever it takes place. Near the top of most lists are bugs: biters and stingers to be avoided or from which to recover. Close behind them are the dangers and hassles of too much sun and exposure to poisonous plants.

Insects

The world is home to more than one million species of insects, North America to about 90,000, according to the experts at the Tender Corporation, which makes insect repellents and related products. Collectively, the world's insects weigh about the same as the world's people.

Flies

Earth has more than 60,000 species of flies. Most troublesome are house, horse, deer, bot, blow, black, and fruit flies. Mosquitoes, gnats, and midges are flies, too, but Tender puts them in a class of their own. Black flies are drawn to dark, moving objects. Dress in light colored clothes. Horse, house, and other flies hang around horses and cattle. You can keep flies from bugging you by keeping you and the environment clean, staying in breezes, and using a repellent.

Mosquitos

About 200 mosquito species fly across North America, 2,400 worldwide. Regardless of species, only the female bites. She needs a blood meal to continue the line, and bites with a proboscis like a hypodermic needle. Mosquitoes bite most at twilight, and like cool, dark, moist places. Mosquitoes are attracted to blue.

Ticks

Ticks feed mostly on animals, and like mosquitoes, carry disease from victim to victim. In most camping areas they're worst from May through August, especially July.

Chiggers

Chiggers are immature mites that live in sandy soil. They don't bite. They inject an enzyme that breaks down skin cells, and then they ingest the partly digested cells. They drop to the ground but

Natrapel uses citronella, not DEET, to keep biting insects away.

A line of DEET-free products

leave an itchy, irritated skin that can last more than a week, with swelling, redness, and scabs.

Ants

Fire ants are common in the Southwest and South. They came here from South America after World War II, and many people are allergic to their bite. Unfortunately you won't often get one bite; you'll get usually ten, twenty, or more.

Fleas

Of the 2,000 known species of fleas, twenty species bite humans. Flea bites usually come in clusters, most often around ankles and legs, and they itch like crazy.

Avoid 'em

General pest avoidance tricks include avoiding scented soaps, lotions, and shampoos, which can attract bugs and bees. Cover skin with clothing. We can repel many types of biting insects, too, such as mosquitoes, ticks, ants, and an industry has

grown around this notion.

If you camp, you'll encounter insect pests. There are great ways available to avoid them, though, and effective ways to deal with their bites and stings if you don't.

Bites and Stripes

Insects torment campers in two ways: by stinging or biting. Stinging insects inject poison that brings pain. To people allergic to their stings, they can bring worse. Biting insects, though, are probably responsible for more ruined camping trips than are their stinging cousins. Mosquitoes, black flies, ticks are tops on the list of things campers hate.

Bugs come in many sizes and shapes, and with many attack styles. Bees and wasps, for example, sting. Short of avoidance, there's not much we can do about them. Once they've stung, we can best deal with it by removing the stinger, flicking it out of the skin with a credit card or similar item, rather than grasping the stinger and maybe injecting more venom.

Some repellents keep insects at bay. Some kill them. We'll get to that in a minute.

Hard to Beat DEET

To keep biting insects from biting your skin, you're probably going to rely on a chemical called N,N-diethyl-meta-toluamide, better known as DEET. It was developed by the U.S. Department of

Agriculture in the 1940s, and remains the top-ranked bug-repellent. It works by creating a chemical zone above your skin that confuses any biting flies aloft in search of a meal.

You might not find "DEET" on repellent ingredient labels, though. The EPA, which regulates the products, requires the full name, which can be presented in one of three forms: N,N diethyl-m-toluamide; N,N,diethyl m toluamide; or n,n,diethyl-m-toluamide.

Nothing has beaten DEET at baffling bugs yet, although in recent years there's been increasing concern that its overuse, especially by youngsters, can be a health threat. DEET is absorbed through the skin and into the bloodstream. Skin rashes and neurological reactions have been reported. Most experts now suggest using the least amount of DEET necessary to get the job done, which makes label reading an important pre-trip concern.

You can purchase insect repellents in spray, lotion, cream or wax stick form. DEET-based repellents can have as little as 8-percent DEET (the rest of the product is scents, propellants, lotion bases, and other inert ingredients), or as much as 95 percent. The goal is to find the one most convenient for you, in the lowest level of DEET that will handle the pests at hand. Some experts recommend that adults use a DEET-based repellent that carries the concentration at levels of 40 percent or less, and that children use repellents at half that strength or less.

Stronger repellents do work a bit longer, but not, experts say, in proportion to their additional strength. Studies have shown that using lower strength DEET, and reapplying it when it begins to fail, can provide the same protection as a stronger solution with a lower overall skin exposure to DEET.

Natural Alternatives

For kids, some makers offer repellents that use active ingredients other than DEET to keep bugs away. Citronella is a natural and commonly used ingredient, and it is much milder on children's skin, although it loses its effectiveness quickly. A compromise is to use DEET on kids' clothes, testing first to make sure it won't harm the garments, then apply a citronella repellent to their skin, reapplying it as necessary.

Ticks

DEET on your skin also repels ticks, but not well enough to ensure you won't get bitten by one of these disease-spreading pests.

Ticks don't fly or jump. They linger on vegetation and wait for a meal to pass. Brush a blade of grass, and you may pick up a hitch-hiking tick. If it's had a meal from an infected animal or person, it can then transmit a disease to you.

A tick only eats three blood meals in its lifetime: at nymph, larvae, and adult stages. It can carry disease from one victim to the next.

Lyme Disease

Many diseases are transmitted by deer ticks. One of the most prominent in recent years is Lyme disease, which reveals itself days to weeks after a bite by an infected tick. It often shows first as a small reddish spot at the site of the bite. A rash may appear, often in a bull's-eye pattern. Symptoms include chills, fatigue, headache, and joint and muscle aches. Untreated, Lyme disease can cause arthritic joint inflammation, neurological problems, and heart ailments. It is most often treated with antibiotics as soon as the disease appears.

Ticks carry other diseases, too, such as Rocky Mountain spotted fever, tularemia, Human ehrlichiosis, and others.

Tick Tricks

Obviously, efforts to avoid ticks make a lot of sense.

If you'll be camping in tick country, heavy artillery is in order. One approach is applying

Pro-Tick Remedy by SCS

DEET directly to clothing, at stronger levels. Another is netted clothing treated with strong DEET preparations. A third is a different chemical, entirely, one called *permethrin*.

Permethrin kills ticks on contact, and also kills mosquitoes and biting flies. This chemical was developed as a synthetic version of pyrethrin, the chemical produced by chrysanthemum plants to keep insects at bay.

Permethrin is extremely effective at keeping mosquitoes, as well as ticks, away. Add some DEET on your skin, one company says, and almost every mosquito will stay away. Permethrin breaks down on contact with skin, but perseveres on clothing and fabric used in camping gear. It keeps working for about two weeks, even through a washing or two. While DEET mainly confuses mosquitoes and other insects, permethrin kills the bugs that land on it. It also has repellent qualities.

Anti-Tick Attire

Beyond permethrin, you can keep ticks off by tucking your pantlegs into boots or socks, staying in the center of hiking paths and away from tall grass, and inspecting yourself and others for ticks after each outing.

Some experts suggest wearing light-color clothes to make it easier to spot a tick climbing around looking for access to your skin.

After the Bite

Found one, and it's already bitten? Remove it. It usually takes twenty-four hours for a tick to inject the saliva that carries disease. It expels saliva to help it remove its mouth parts from the wound, and that's at the end of its blood meal. The saliva carries most of the disease danger. That's why you don't just want to tug a tick off, or squeeze it with tweezers, or cover it with grease. That could increase the chances of it injecting Lyme organisms into your system.

Instead, using pointed tweezers or a special tool such as described below, grasp the tick as close to the skin as you can and apply gentle, steady, upward pressure until it pops free. Then apply rubbing alcohol or povidine iodine to disinfect the wound.

Some experts advise keeping a tick if it's had some time to feed upon you, so that it can be identified by an expert later. Ticks dry quickly, though, making it nearly impossible to identify one unless you keep it in a sealed container with a moist paper towel, or preserve it with rubbing alcohol.

Sun Sense

It's not just that we know more about the dangers of sunburn than we once did. It's that those dangers appear greater now than they did then.

As the Earth's ozone layer deteriorates, it allows more ultraviolet energy from the sun to reach us. Those rays age the skin and boost the odds of skin cancer.

Not Kid Stuff

Those risks are especially high for kids, because experts say about three-fourths of a lifetime's sun-caused skin damage takes place before we're 18 years old. And we can't turn back that solar clock. Some experts say one blistering sunburn as a kid can result in double the danger of getting skin cancer later.

There are two forms of ultraviolet rays from the sun: Ultraviolet B (UV-B) and Ultraviolet A (UV-A).

UV-B is stronger in summer, when it causes sunburn and increases the risk of skin cancer. It is most directly responsible for burning the skin.

UV-A penetrates deep where it causes sunburn, skin cancer, and premature aging of the skin. It amplifies the damage caused by UV-B.

Avoid the UV

There are several ways to protect against sunburn. One is to avoid being outdoors at midday—10 A.M. to 3 P.M—when sun rays are the strongest.

Maybe you can schedule museum visits and other car-camping activities for the middle of the day. On many camping trips, however, the entire day is spent outdoors. You can protect yourself then by dressing in clothing made of tightly-woven fabrics.

Some clothing makers even advertise the sun protection factor (SPF) of clothing. That rating system is more often associated with sun-blocking lotions and gels for bare skin. Tightly woven fabrics are reported to provide an SPF rating of 30 or more. SPF 30 means that your exposure to the sun for thirty minutes with the protection is the same as one minute without it.

A wide-brimmed hat shields the face and ears from some of the sunlight. One report indicated a reduction of skin cancer risk of 40 percent, just by wearing a hat with a 4-inch brim. Most skin cancers, it said, develop on the head and neck; one-third of all of them on the nose. The most protective clothing is made of tightly woven and thicker fabric, in darker colors.

Sunproof Kids

Children should be protected against sunburn, even on cloudy days. The people at Tender Corporation suggest dressing kids in clothing made of tightly woven fabric and protecting exposed skin with a water-resistant or waterproof sunscreen with a SPF factor of at least 15.

(courtesy Custom Outdoor Products)

Sunsect sunscreen insect repellent

Protect kids' eyes, too, with child-size sunglasses with UV protection.

Sunscreens and glasses should both make it clear they guard against UV-B and UV-A.

Plant Problems

Only people enjoy the sport of camping. Only they escape their regular routines for romps in the outdoors. Only they suffer from exposure to poison ivy, poison oak, and poison sumac.

The problem within these plants is an oil called urushiol, which causes allergic reactions in most people. You can run into trouble touching the plants or even petting dogs or cats that have played in it. Some experts say you can break out after touching clothing or garden tools that touched it years before. Urushiol can even be carried on smoke particles, and the reaction could be a serious one in your lungs.

First aid? If you think you've messed with poison ivy, poison oak, or poison sumac, wash the skin area with rubbing alcohol. Then take a long shower.

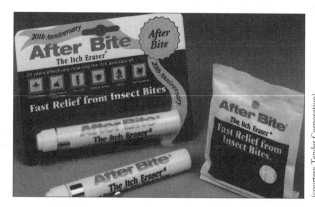

The pain of bites and stings can be soothed with After Bite.

Products/Services

Coulston's Duranon Tick Repellent is made only for application to clothing. It is ineffective in repelling insects when applied to the skin, where it breaks down quickly. A clothing application of its active ingredient, permethrin, is said to be effective against ticks and mosquitoes for two full weeks, even through two launderings. Company personnel say the treatment is odorless in spraying and after drying, and is non-staining, non-greasy, and compatible with all clothing, fabrics, and equipment. One 6-ounce pressurized spray can treat two complete sets of outdoor clothing, the company says.

Custom Outdoor Products makes Sunsect, which protects against insects and sunburn with one product. Its formulation traps DEET and suspends it on top of the skin. That keeps more of the chemical from being absorbed by the skin, reducing the amount needed for protection. Sunsect's DEET content is 20 percent.

Sunsect also claims up to eight hours of waterproof and sweat-proof protection, UV-A and UV-B sunscreen protection that is PABA free, with an SPF of 15.

A kids' Sunsect product has a 9.5-percent DEET content and SPF of 30.

Hypo-allergenic Sunsect and Sunsect for Kids have aloe vera to moisturize skin.

Sawyer Products has assembled a wealth of

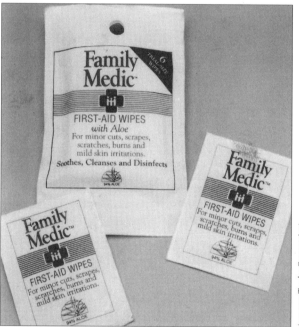

Family Medic first aid wipes

health information in its spiral-bound *Sawyer Solutions: A Practical Guide to Outdoor Protection* ($9.99). The book focuses on biting flies, stinging insects, sun exposure, poisonous plants, and other outdoor hazards. In each category it describes the creature or force, its effect on people, and how to avoid or recover from it. It's perfect for the glove compartment of a camper's car, along with first-aid products such as those manufactured by Sawyer.

Sawyer also makes a full line of insect repellents and sunscreens.

SCS's Pro-Tick Remedy allows the user to position the tick within the device's V-shaped notch and lift it off. It is small and convenient to carry, ruggedly made of stainless steel, dependable with no moving parts, affordable, and easy to use.

Shoo Bug jackets ($29) and pants ($25) are treated with a DEET-based insect repellent. Sold separately in storage bags, they provide as many as 1,000 hours of protection against mosquitoes, chiggers, black flies, and ticks before the garments need retreatment. When they do, 2-ounce bottles of retreatment ($3.99) are available. Shoo-Bug togs pull on over regular clothing. They're made of a wide-mesh cotton-polyester fabric, so they remain comfortable even on those hot muggy days when bug problems seem the worst.

Tender Corporation is the maker of Ben's Max, with 95-percent DEET, for bug infested areas or where Lyme disease is a concern. Ben's Backyard formula is 23-percent DEET, for family use in areas of light bug infestation.

Tender also offers Bug Armor, an olive-colored mesh suit with hooded jacket and pants "charged" with Ben's Max. It provides complete insect protection without application of repellent directly on the skin, holding its charge for several months when kept in its own storage bag.

Tender's Natrapel is a citronella-based product that provides insect protection for up to two hours. It is best for children in areas without heavy bug infestation, say company experts. It contains 10-percent citronella, compared to other brands with one-twentieth that amount.

Tender's After Bite is a treatment with ammonia hydroxide and mineral oil to stop the itch of bites and pain of stings. That helps avoid the threat of secondary infection that can result from scratching a bite or sting.

Family Medic First Aid Treatment, with 80-percent aloe, disinfects and relieves pain for all minor first-aid needs. It comes in a ½-ounce travel vial, a plastic package of six disposable towelettes, and a 4-ounce pump spray.

Family Medic AfterBurn Gel contains 95-percent aloe and the anesthetic lidocaine, for instant relief from sunburn or windburn.

Wisconsin Pharmacal Company offers several ways to beat the bugs in its Repel line. Its own IPF (insect protection factor) designation system identifies the DEET content of its repellents. Repel offers

Where To Go?

The Recreation Vehicle Industry Association (RVIA), offers these tips on picking a camping destination:

- Purchase or borrow one of the many national campground directories available at bookstores or libraries; informative guides are also often available to members of insurance company clubs such as AAA and Allstate.
- Contact individual federal or state parks, forests, or other public lands for information on their campsites and nearby private campgrounds.
- Write to travel and tourism bureaus for area camping information. (For a free list of state travel directors, send a self-addressed, stamped envelope to the Travel Industry Association of America, 1100 New York Ave., Northwest, Suite 450, Washington, D.C.)
- Join RV and camping clubs and contact state campground associations to receive newsletters and updates.
- Call (800) 47–SUNNY toll-free for RVIA's free, comprehensive camping vacation planner, or write to Go Camping America, P.O. Box 2669, Department 23, Reston, VA 22090.

five concentrations: IPF 7, 15, 18, 20, and 27. One lotion combines an IPF 20 with a sun block of SPF 15. Repellents are available in lotion, gel, pump spray, and aerosol.

Repel 100 is 100-percent DEET, for use in the most extreme conditions.

Repel's Permanone is an aerosol permethrin-based product. Sprayed on clothing, it provides protection for two weeks. A Repel IPF product, applied to the skin, adds to the defense.

For wilderness travel, Repel offers mosquito nets in three sizes.

Sources

Coulston Products, Inc.
P.O. Box 30
Easton, PA 18044–0030
(215) 253–0167

Custom Outdoor Products
1007 Dothan Road
Bainbridge, GA 31717
(912) 248–0678

Sawyer Products
P.O. Box 188
Safety Harbor, FL 34695
(800) 940–4464

SCS, Ltd.
P.O. Box 573
Stony Point, NY 10980
(800) 749–8425
Web site: http:\\iypn.com\scs
E-mail: scs@mne.net

Shoo Bug
Cole Outdoor Products
P.O. Box 81336
Lincoln, NE 68501
(888) SHOO–BUG
Fax: (402) 488–2321

Tender Corporation
P.O. Box 290
Littleton Industrial Park
Littleton, NH 03561
(800) 258–4696

Wisconsin Pharmacal Co.
1 Repel Road, P.O. Box 198
Jackson, WI 53037
(800) 558–6614
(414) 677–9000

Chapter 10
Good Housekeeping

The camper is judged by how little impact he or she has on the special place visited. There are ways to keep that impact minimal, plus tips on privacy, quiet, handling problems, helping other campers, and more. Here are some of them.

No Trace!

Some people just can't move through their world without leaving a mark: graffiti on building walls, initials carved in trees, names in lights. Others, campers among them, pride themselves on

A clean camp is a happy and healthy camp.

Camping Trivia Quiz

By KOA

How much do you really know about camping? Most of us know the basics: campfire building, marshmallow toasting, and a few other necessary outdoor skills. But how much do we know about how the camping craze got started?

To find out your "Camping IQ," try your luck with the following trivia quiz. If you don't know the answer, give it your best guess. The correct answers follow the quiz.

Good luck!

1) An early nickname for campers who traveled by car was:
   a. Road Warriors
   b. Tin Can Tourists
   c. Car Campers
   d. Tent Travelers

2) In 1914, The Coleman Company produced its first:
   a. lantern
   b. stove
   c. cooler
   d. tent

3) The president of the Packard Motor Car Company had a camping vehicle built on a Packard automobile chassis in:
   a. 1910
   b. 1915
   c. 1922
   d. 1935

4) Henry Ford and Harvey Firestone were part of a group of famous auto campers that also included:
   a. Teddy Roosevelt
   b. Melville Ferguson
   c. Thomas Edison
   d. Emily Post

5) When this U.S. President went on an auto camping outing, it seemed that "everyone was doing it."
   a. Teddy Roosevelt
   b. Warren Harding
   c. Herbert Hoover
   d. Woodrow Wilson

6) The original travel vehicles were either owner-built or custom-built for a purchaser. The first model of RVs to be mass-produced on an assembly line were:
   a. motorhomes
   b. travel trailers

c. fifth-wheels
    d. folding tent trailers

7) According to the *New York Times,* how many people camped in 1922?
    a. 5 million
    b. 7 million
    c. 10 million
    d. 15 million

8) Like travel trailers, early motorhomes were custom-built models. The first manufactured Type A motorhome was built in:
    a. 1956
    b. 1960
    c. 1964
    d. 1968

9) The first KOA Kampground opened in Billings, Montana in:
    a. 1962
    b. 1965
    c. 1968
    d. 1970

10) Today, campers—tenters, RVers and cabin campers—number roughly:
    a. 42 million
    b. 50 million
    c. 58 million
    d. 64 million

Now that you've finished, are you stumped or smug? If you're stumped, continue reading; here are the correct answers:

1) b. An early nickname for campers who traveled by car was Tin Can Tourists.

2) a. The Coleman Company was founded in 1899 to produce gas lamps for residential and commercial use. Coleman entered the camping market in 1914 with the introduction of the first Coleman lantern, which was followed by the Coleman stove in 1923, the Coleman cooler in 1954, and Coleman's first tents in 1965.

3) b. Mr. Joyce, then president of Packard Motor Car Company, had a camping vehicle built on a Packard chassis in 1915. The vehicle provided eating, sleeping, and cooking facilities for two people.

4) c. Thomas Edison joined Henry Ford, Harvey Firestone, and naturalist John Burroughs for an auto camping trip Burroughs described as "a welcome escape from luxuries that alienated modern man from 'first principles.'" (Emily Post, however, chronicled her auto camping experiences with her son, E.M., in the book, *By Motor to the Golden Gate.)*

5) b. In 1921, the illustrious auto camping group that included Henry Ford, Thomas Edison, and Harvey Firestone was joined for an outing by President Warren G. Harding.

6) d. The earliest record of factory assembly-line RV production was in 1926 at the Chenango Camp Trailer Company in Norwich, New York; the product was folding tent trailers.

7) d. According to *The New York Times*, there were 15 million campers in 1922, most of whom slept on cots, in tents, or in "newfangled houses on wheels."

8) b. In 1960, the Frank Motor Home was the first successful attempt by manufacturers to produce Type A motorhomes. The vehicles were more commonly known as Dodge Motor Homes because they were built on Dodge chassis; the line was later known as Travco due to changes in ownership.

9) a. The first KOA Kampground opened in Billings, Montana, in 1962 as a "travelers' oasis" for people traveling to and from the Seattle World's Fair.

10) d. Today, there are roughly 64 million camping enthusiasts who regularly escape to the great outdoors to camp in tents, RVs, or cabins.

moving through their world, the natural world that is, without leaving a trace.

No-trace camping is an art form. Books have been written, classes organized and taught, on how to visit and area and leave no sign of the visit.

Almost every national park and wilderness area goes to great lengths to explain camping principles that leave the world none the worse for your visit. Many of the tips related here come from a brochure distributed by Voyageurs National Park in Minnesota. Other suggestions come from the **Izaak Walton League,** which works to boost ethical behavior outdoors.

No—Trace Tips

Going camping, and want to leave no trace? Follow these guidelines:

Keep the size of your group small. Your camping group can pitch its tents within the space available at campsites, and there'll be less noise, too, which will boost everyone's enjoyment.

Try to schedule your visits during times of the year when crowds are slimmer. Seasonal trends vary by location; managers of the campground and area can often provide tips for selecting overlooked visiting times.

If you need lights, bring appliances that are reliable and quiet. You don't need a noisy generator and 110-volt lights. Campers who use small flashlights and only when absolutely necessary, or no lights at all, are often pleasantly surprised both by how well they adapt to the natural world after dark and by how much they enjoy it.

Save Those Sites

If you bring in coolers, use the smallest you need, and use those that are easy to carry. You won't be tempted to drag them over delicate areas.

Use campsites that already exist. Even pitching a tent one night has an impact on vegetation and soils. We preserve the wild area we visit when we sacrifice a few areas for campsites and avoid the rest.

If you must camp on a new site, choose one where you're not trampling plants, and make it at least 200 feet from water.

Clean up a messy site. Don't dig or trench in camp. Wearing smooth-soled shoes will minimize the mark you leave.

Wash yourself and your dishes at least 200 feet from water. Strain the dishwater, scatter it, and put the food debris with trash to avoid attracting bears and other animals.

Small pieces of wood make the best campfire.

Hygiene

Minimize the effects of the area on you. Filter your drinking through a filter rated at 0.4 microns or smaller, or boil the water (see Chapter 4).

At a site with no bathroom facilities, dig a cat hole in the top few inches of soil, at least 200 feet from water and the campsite. Burn or pack out toilet paper. If you brought it in; bring it out. That includes feminine hygiene products, trash, and garbage.

Leave pets home or keep them on a leash no longer than 6 feet. Remove and dispose of dog feces as you would human feces.

Cleaning and Cooking

Bring a stove for cooking, even if you expect to cook over wood. Years of campfires have left fuel wood scarce in many areas.

Use common sense and follow area rules if you catch and clean fish. Some areas advise burying entrails, others advise placing them on rocks for seagulls or sinking them in deep water far from shore. Rules vary, too. In Minnesota, for example, suggestions from Voyageurs National Park (deep water) and the Boundary Waters Canoe Area Wilderness (shoreline rocks) urge you to violate state law (can't place offal on shoreline or in water.) Go figure. Remember, though, that bears and other scavengers may be drawn to fish remains.

Bear-proof your camp. Hang all food packs at least 10 feet off the ground, 4 feet from a tree trunk, and 4 feet beneath a limb. If campgrounds provide bear-proof food containers, use them.

Ways on Water

Even canoeists and small boaters can impact their watery environments. An article in The Izaak Walton League's *Outdoor Ethics* newsletter suggests that canoeists avoid paddling through emergent aquatic plants, those that rise to the top of the water. If you can't help moving through them, have each craft follow the one ahead of it to minimize

Where fires are allowed, they add to a camp.

the disturbance.

When landing a canoe, pick a sandy or rocky spot if possible, so you do not disturb shoreline wetlands.

Trail Tricks

On trails, the League suggests you wear the lightest shoe you can, with smooth rather than lugged soles if possible. Walk in single file to keep the trail narrow. Stay on the trail on switchbacks; don't speed erosion by taking or creating shortcuts.

Walk through mud holes instead of around them, to avoid enlarging the quagmire.

Fire!

Perhaps no camping discussion gets as heated as one that concerns fire. For many, a campfire is a basic part of the tradition. For others, fire is to be avoided for its danger, unsightly remains, and drain on wood resources. It all seems to depend where you're camping.

At many of the campgrounds we visit, every

Journal Entry: A Gracious (Campground) Host

Gene Gilson was finally doing what he'd seen hundreds of people do in the past month: leaving Muskallonge State Park along Michigan's Lake Superior shoreline.

Where most of those other people camped a week or ten days and headed home, Gilson had been here for thirty days. And instead of home, he was heading for another park, for another thirty-day hitch.

Gilson is a campground host, a voluntary position the Michigan Department of Natural Resources' (DNR) Parks and Recreation Division uses to make its parks more friendly. Hosts' only pay is free camping, and sometimes their choice of campsites. Gilson, a three-year veteran of the program, had several park postings under his belt.

A campground host, greets campers, directs visitors, explains fees, assists in park activities, checks camper registrations, and provides information to visitors. Some even hold campfire sing-alongs or berry-picking outings. There are sometimes routine maintenance tasks, too.

"With me," said Gilson, relaxing at a camper's picnic table, "my number one priority is making sure there's toilet paper in the bathroom."

That, any camper will tell you, is important. It can be a challenge, too, when a male campground host needs to replenish the paper in the women's bathroom.

"One time at the Straits State Park I thought I would get it done at night, so at midnight I waited outside. I waited forty-five minutes. Three women would go in, two would come out. I kept track until I knew it was empty. Then I went in and locked the door from the inside, replaced eight rolls of paper in five minutes, and when I unlocked the door there were six women waiting to get in. At 1 A.M. in the morning. A couple of them were mad."

What else does the host do?

"I walk around periodically and keep my eyes open, make sure everybody goes by the rules. If not, I tell them what the rules are. I tell them one time. If that doesn't work I tell the (DNR) people at the contact station, and they take care of it. They warn people three times, then they make them leave the park. I've seen that happen."

Sometimes the presence of a host seems to ward off problems.

"Kids see the hat and badge and they think: hey, it's a ranger," said Gilson. "I'm not a ranger. I have no law enforcement authority. But they see me and think that, and they're more apt to do what they're supposed to do."

Most host tasks are pleasant, such as the coffee break Gilson holds one morning each week. Many nights he plays his guitar at his own campsite, and he's always ready to move to a camping group's fire by request for a sing-along.

At the time we spoke, the previous week's programs included a sand castle building contest, in which small groups fashioned creations such as a butterfly with Lake Superior stone wings, a turtle returning to the "sea" with young turtles hatching from eggs behind her, and a pair of Pokey Little Puppies with stone claws and noses.

The Adventure Ranger naturalist asked Gilson to be a judge, "and I agreed. I didn't figure there'd be that much down there. But when I got to the bottom of the steps (to Lake Superior) and saw the beautiful things they had made, I wanted to turn around and walk away. Judging was hard."

Leaving Muskallonge would be hard for Gilson, too. "I like the setting and I like the people. I've made some super friends, and it chokes me up when they have to go."

"It's a good place to camp free," said Gilson. "I enjoy being outdoors, and I enjoy being with people."

site has a campfire pit, and fires have been so popular for so long that there's literally no dead and downed wood nearby. Concessionaires sell campers bundles of sawmill waste wood. Sometimes it's dry and burns beautifully, sometimes it was standing timber the week before, and it smolders stubbornly. It's still a campfire, though, so we toast marshmallows, poke at the coals, and dream campfire dreams around it.

In other settings we've done all our cooking over a cheery wood fire fed with wood we've gathered ourselves.

In yet other wilderness settings open fires are banned, so we have cooked our meals on a handy backpacking stove.

Sometimes it's your choice to have a fire or not. Sometimes the rules dictate.

To Build a Fire

If you're building a fire, begin by clearing out an area around the spot, so that duff and other forest material can't catch flame and spread. Use an existing fire area if possible, a ring, pit, or scar that's already there. If you must use a new location, a fire pit can be dug and carefully refilled when you're done with the fire and certain that it's out. Another good option is a mound fire built on mineral soil, on a solid base such as rock. The soil keeps the rock from scorching; the two protect the organic material on the forest floor.

If the weather has been generally dry for a few days, gather sticks less than a quarter-inch in diameter. If you only have larger pieces available, shave off some smaller ones with a knife. If it's been rainy, look under logs for dry wood. Light the small pieces, then add larger ones. Large logs make dreamy fires; medium-size wood makes it easier to add a bit to boost cooking temperatures slightly.

Whatever kind of fire, this rule remains in effect: never leave a fire until you've drowned it completely with water.

"Tread Lightly!"

In 1985 a U.S. Forest Service task force gathered to devise ways to deal with the increase of recreational visitors, especially motorized visitors, to public lands. As a consequence the concept of *Tread Lightly!* was developed; a long-term, informative program to increase public awareness that recreationists must take special care of lands if opportunities are to continue.

Soon after the Forest Service developed the program, the Bureau of Land Management, with its vast Western U.S. land holdings, adopted it. American corporations joined, too, and the government decided it was logical to transfer the program's management to the private sector. Thus, in 1990, about fifty companies and organizations founded the nonprofit organization *Tread Lightly!,* Inc.

Some basic principles involved in being environmentally responsible are summarized in the *Tread Lightly!* pledge:

Travel only on designated routes
Respect the rights of others
Educate yourself
Avoid stream banks, meadows, wildlife, etc.
Drive and travel responsibly

Video Vision

Adventures for a Lifetime: A Guide to Low Impact Camping ($19), is a new instructional video designed to teach beginning and experienced campers better base and backcountry camping techniques, emphasizing low-impact or leave-no-trace camping methods.

The video, produced by **Brewster Video Productions**, follows a vacationing family into some of the most beautiful regions of Montana's backcountry. Along the way, outdoor professionals teach family members how to select equipment, pick a campsite, make camp, cook, sleep, and perform other camping activities.

The video was produced in association with the Partnership For The Outdoors, a group including Coleman, JanSport, DuPont, General Ecology, Vasque, and other companies, competing firms joining in efforts to create, maintain, and enjoy a better environment. Fifty percent of the proceeds from the video's sales go to the American Hiking Society and the Outdoor Recreation Coalition of America, two nonprofit groups dedicated to preserving wilderness areas.

Sources

Adventures For A Lifetime
Brewster Video
1399 East 28th Street
Long Beach, CA 90804
(800) 748–1173

Tread Lightly! **Inc.**
298 24th Street, Suite 325
Ogden, UT 84401
(801) 627–0077
Fax: (801) 621–8633

Izaak Walton League of America, Inc.
707 Conservation Lane
Gaithersburg, MD 20878–2983
(301) 548–0150
Fax: (301) 548–0146

Chapter 11
Camping at the Extremes

Summer is camping season. School's out, beaches are friendly, attractions are open and flourishing. There's fine camping available year round, though, and some of my favorite stays have been in places and during seasons the crowds missed. It takes some extra planning and some special equipment, but hiking under conditions some call marginal, or even extreme, can offer special benefits.

Water Worries

Camping in deserts and other hot environments require special considerations. Top among them is water: finding, carrying, and drinking enough of it.

Some desert travelers count on finding water at remembered or recommended springs. That's chancy, because these natural features change from year to year. If you do use spring water, make sure you filter, purify, or boil it (see Chapter 3). Check with local experts, too, to make sure there's no danger from heavy metals or other chemical contamination.

Dry environments can turn very wet very quickly. Flash floods are always a threat to a desert traveler. If storm clouds threaten, make sure you quickly get out of watercourses such as canyons.

You need special protection from the sun in desert environments. Wide-brimmed hats, long sleeve shirts, long pants, and sunscreen must all match this harsh world (see Chapter 9).

Desert settings—here, Utah's redrock country—provide special views.

Journal Entry October 1993: Camping at the Margins

It gets cold up here, several thousand feet above sea level. Alpine cold balances the heat the autumn desert still boasts: It is 90 degrees Fahrenheit or more on the desert floor every day, a sweat-forming heat that makes filling water jugs an ever-present concern. The desert, whose lizards have underbodies of blue, whose sandstone walls bear petroglyphs left in impossible places centuries ago.

That's the desert. Yesterday's Utah desert, and perhaps today's. But this Utah mountain morning hangs on cold. Next to the aspen-clad hillside is a mountain top bare except for a slab of snow along one side. Is it a leftover from last winter's white bounty? Or a pledge of watery wafers to come? No one seems to know.

Three mule deer meander through the camp this early morning, two for-sure does and one whose head is never clearly seen. It might be antlered. They're browsing on brush in the understory beneath the 16-inch-thick poplars. The deer munch, and the occasional slamming car door or yapping dog at the far end of camp doesn't seem to bother them much. Finally, full or frightened, they dance off on stiff legs.

I slow-dance off on stiff legs later. Up through aspens, to pine, to rock slide, past the little meadow with its remnants of a cabin, with a view down through a gunsight notch into a chunk of Utah's Red Rock desert country.

Then up again, always up, painfully up, through more bright yellow poplars. Walk fifty steps, rest these Midwestern lungs, then up another one hundred steps. Count the steps, argue with myself about how many to take this time. Wait for the head to quit banging. Then up another fifty and quit. Miners Basin, to which the sign points, will wait for another day, or more likely, another hiker.

The lungs should fill more easily walking back down, I can't say for sure, so carefully do I watch each step on the broken rock trail. Insteps burn, knees scream, and calves ache.

At the bottom of the trail a retired lady looking for a trail asks about this one. I'm told it's quite steep, she says. It's a great way to make a winterish day feel summerish, I tell her. She nods.

Winter Camping

John Johnson, in a backpacking workshop, shows slides of a New Year's Eve spent in a backpack/ski camp with temperatures dropping to 0 degrees Fahrenheit.

The veteran backpacker doesn't talk much about the cold drawbacks of winter camping, though. He talks about its big advantages. You don't have to hike, he says. You can move on cross-country skis or snowshoes. You don't need to carry heavy packs, he says. You can pull large loads, on sleds.

Winter camping does require a three- or four-season tent, which means it's stout and well-engineered enough to withstand the wind and snow that season can bring (see Chapter 2).

If you do carry a pack while skiing or snowshoeing, you're best advised to make it an internal frame pack, because it's narrower, and has a lower, better balancing center of gravity (see Chapter 3).

If camping on snow, prepare a campsite by stomping it down with your snowshoes, skis, or sled. That creates a firm platform on which you can pitch a tent.

Water, always a concern to the camper, is generally abundant through snow. Melting snow can be a hassle, though, so it's best to find a source of liquid water. If not, melt the snow very slowly to avoid scorching the pan.

Keep yourself warm by eating plenty of high-energy food and make sure you drink plenty of water.

Dress for Success

Dressing in layers is more important than ever in winter. Make sure you wear wicking layers near the skin, insulating layers above it, and windproof or waterproof layers on the outside. Change layer arrangements as weather conditions and activity levels change.

Today's boots offer comfort undreamed of just a few years ago. Footgear is offered that keeps toes toasty to 100 below. Match your boots to the activity level: pac boots are fine if driving to a site, then milling about on the ice, fishing. Lighter boots work better if you're on the move, though.

Inside the boots you can add comfort with heavyweight rag socks made of wool and stretch nylon or other specialty materials.

Gaiters, sleeves that fit over the bottom of trousers and the tops of boots, keep snow from tumbling into boots and melting.

RVs Warm Home for Winter Camping

Recreation vehicles are perfect for winter camping, according to the Recreation Vehicle Industry Association, which has published a booklet entitled, *Wintertime RV Use and Maintenance* ($2).

The booklet offers advice on how to prepare for a winter RV camping trip, an equipment checklist, and information on winter maintenance and storage. Among tips for RV travel in cold weather:

- Heating an RV in the winter requires an adequate gas supply. Liquid propane gas tanks should be large enough for extended cold-weather trips. RVers should make sure their unit uses propane, not butane, because butane will not work in tempera-

tures below freezing.
- Winter campers should select a sunny campsite—not a shady one—near a wind break if possible. Park with either the front or rear of the RV into the wind. If possible make reservations ahead of time to make sure the campground is open year-round. Some year-round campgrounds even offer such payoffs as hot tubs and saunas, perfect for driving out the winter chill.
- Keep driving speeds down on icy roads. Frequently check the "feel" of the road when no other vehicles are near to determine limits for safe acceleration and braking.

Products/Services

Brunton was thinking about the extremes when it created its Elite kit ($68), which includes its Model 8040 map compass, four survival cards with outdoor survival data, thermometer (minus 200–1,200 degrees Fahrenheit), wind speed and wind-chill chart, range finder, clinometer, and nylon case.

A smaller Survival Kit includes three waterproof cards with essential outdoor survival information, 2.5 x fresnel lens for fire starting, and a floating disc compass.

B-West Outdoor Specialties' line of clothing and camping items from Africa includes breathable cotton Men's Safari Trousers ($49), Short and Long Sleeve Safari Shirts ($39–$49), Safari Shorts ($39), Safari Vest ($69), and Knee Length and Long Safari Skirts ($29–$49). Pith helmets ($49) provide protection from the sun.

Granite Gear makes hats, mittens, and gloves especially for the winter wanderer. The company created its own Bombshell and Bombshell Plus fabrics. Bombshell fabric is made of two layers with a waterproof, breathable coating. Bombshell Plus is three layers, waterproof and breathable. The outer shell of each is a 330-denier Cordura/Supplex blend. The inner membrane technology is from SympaTex, protected by an inner liner of tricot fabric.

Snowcountry Gloves are anatomically cut for a pre-curved fit. They feature a full length, removable liner, made of Dyersburg E.C.O. fleece. The closure is a ¾-inch wrist cinch and one-handed bungee closure at the top of the gauntlet. Lutsen Mountain Mitts have a double liner of E.C.O. fleece, and the same closures as the gloves.

Granite Gear's North Shore Hat is insulated with Dyersburg E.C.O. fleece and covered with Bombshell fabric. It can be worn as a cap or secured under the chin for full coverage. The North Shore Hat is similar, but the top is fleece all the way through to allow body moisture to escape.

MPI's Space-brand Emergency Blanket provides protection from heat, wind, or cold. It weighs just 2 ounces, but the thin polyester film with vapor-deposited aluminum coating has a tensile strength of 12,500 pounds per square inch.

The metal and polyester films form a barrier that reflects and retains 80 percent of body heat. The blanket also reflects heat away from the body, and can be used as a ground cover, emergency shelter, solar still, desert sunshade, signal flag, mirror, or for other uses when camping at the extremes.

The Space brand All Weather Blanket has two layers laminated into one, with reinforced corners with grommets and a 1-inch vinyl binding sewn onto its edge.

The Space brand Emergency Bag is made from the same material as the Emergency Blanket and is sewn into a full-body coverage bag.

MPI's Emergency Strobe is a small, lightweight, battery-powered strobe light that flashes a light visible for up to 3 miles. It's powered by a single D-cell alkaline battery, and runs for up to sixty hours.

The North Face's new Patrol Pack ($150) is designed specifically for backcountry skiers. The company consulted members of its Extreme Team, heli-skiing guides, ski patrollers, and other professionals while creating this pack. The Patrol Pack features a V-frame suspension and centralized ski-suspension system that provides stability and range of motion. A color-coded vertical lashing system eliminates swaying and makes climbing possible without interference from the skis.

Journal Entry: Deer Camp

Ignore the crunching sounds. No one else heard them, and they're likely the noise of a cheery campfire munching on chunks of oak cut from last year's windfall.

The sounds, though, are from the other direction. Hold up your hand, and *shhh*.

Sure enough, the crunching dance continues, maybe 40 yards out. It moves toward the frozen sand of the forest road and finally out of hearing. One camper leaves the toasty fireside and walks to the road with a flashlight, and he confirms what you suspect.

Deer. Right here, next to camp. The tracks are clear in the skiff of snow that sneaked in at sundown. Hunting all day, you spotted only the bouncing white tails waving you an arrogant good-bye. Now a deer has waltzed right up and looked over your camp.

The deer has inspected your habitat just as you spent the day inspecting his. Your habitat is a deer camp.

Deer camp is where the tales are first told, to become taller, refined, and maybe embellished each night and each year thereafter. It's where meals are cooked and socks dried, where old friends gather for once-a-year visits and families experience once-in-a-lifetime thrills.

Now blend in wood smoke, for there's almost always a campfire smoldering. Add late-night hunting theories and frosty alarm clocks, and you've conjured up part of a deer camp. You're getting closer if you add youngsters on their first hunts and adults fearful of their last, a favorite old hunting spot that's changed slightly from last year, and a long wait at the phone booth in town for the call home to tell of a trophy taken or to ask for a few more days to try.

A deer camp day may begin with a gas lantern illuminating the frosted roof of a camper or tent. The first person up—foolish enough to sleep closest to the alarm clock—must get the first pot of coffee going.

A half-hour later the bacon and most of a dozen eggs are fried. Felt-pac boots are sorted and you pull yours on over toes blanketed in several layers of wool socks. Maybe there's a stack of pancakes or French toast, perhaps some sweet rolls. By the time all the hunters gather around the table there's scant attention paid to the menu anyway. Deer are the special of the day, and everybody's ready for a big helping. Eat, then off.

Those walking to hunting stands together speak in hushed tones, those hiking alone step briskly, hoping to beat the dawn to their hunting area. Most have spent hours in the woods in previous days and weeks, looking for places to hide near areas of heavy deer movement.

Another deer hunting day has begun. Shortly after dawn a shot rings out. You hope it came from the rifle of one of your hunting partners.

Sources

Brunton
620 East Monroe
Riverton, WY 82501
(307) 856–6559
Fax: (307) 856–1840

B-West Outdoor Specialties, Inc.
2425 North Huachuca
Tucson, AZ 85745
(520) 628–1990
Fax: (520) 628–3602

Granite Gear
P.O. Box 278 Industrial Park
Two Harbors, MN 55616
(218) 834–6157
Fax: (218) 834–5545

MPI Outdoors
85 Flagship Drive, Suite D
North Andover, MA 01845–6160
(800) 343–5827
Fax: (508) 685–2992
E-mail: outdoor1@ix.netcom.com
Web site: //www.adventuresports.com/
asap/product/mpi/welcome.htm

Recreation Vehicle Industry Association
P.O. Box 2999
Reston, VA 22090–0999
(703) 620–6003
Fax: (703) 620–5071

The North Face
2013 Farallon Drive
San Leandro, CA 94577
(800) 447–2333

Chapter 12
Canoe Camping

Camping from a canoe carries extra demands and pays extra dividends. Everything you're carrying can be in the water in a moment, so you must prepare differently. Yet the canoe can carry more than you'd want to carry in a backpack, so you have additional food and equipment options. Once at your site, you get the best of a wilderness experience: a camp pitched where walkers and drivers can't go. Here's how to make it happen including advice on special gear and tips from outfitters.

With a canoe you can carry much more than a backpacker can.

Canoe Camping Basics

In some ways, canoe camping offers the best of backpacking and family- or car-camping. Your muscle power is rewarded with scenery not available to everyone, like backpacking. You can generally take quite a bit of equipment, though, as can a driving camper.

Travel Tips

There are a few principles specific to canoe camping, however, and some tips for having a better time afloat and ashore.

- Trust the experts: Many canoe liveries include campouts on their menu of offerings, and some will even rent you the equipment you'll need.
- Don't push the day to the last paddle. End your day early enough to find a campsite and enjoy the surroundings.
- Avoid the temptation to take a houseful of equipment and food. The canoe will hold more than it should!
- Pack everything in waterproof bags. Use commercially made waterproof containers for expensive equipment such as cameras. You can get by with garbage bags for sleeping bags and clothes.
- Wear a life jacket!

Journal Entry: Secret Spots

We met two guys paddling through the Boundary Waters Canoe Area Wilderness in a graceful, beige, Mad River canoe.

"Where are you headed?" we asked, hoping we could find solitude by losing them.

"Here and there," one replied, then adding, "Clear Lake has the big fish."

We were humbled. They saw our plastic canoe and figured we were rubes.

They, of course, were not going to Clear Lake.

We knew, of course, that they weren't going to Clear Lake, and we knew theirs was a clumsy bluff, and we knew that we'd go there, anyway, just because they weren't.

We found the overgrown portage trail to Clear Lake, and unloaded the canoe. I hoisted it above my shoulders, and the 80-pound craft drove my feet 6 inches into the mud. I flopped backwards. We decided to walk the trail first.

It was the right decision. Basketball-size rocks. Crossed logs. A steep ridge. Foot-size holes. We returned to the canoe, reloaded it, and left Clear Lake's big fish for other travelers.

We met those two anglers several more times as we paddled upstream and upwind. They haunted bays and the tailouts of rapids, and they seemed to be catching fish. We walked a long portage on the Kawishiwi River and met them again when we returned to our canoe.

One shouldered the Mad River, which he proudly claimed weighed just 49 pounds, and his partner carried all their gear.

We were left to puzzle over the stringer with four fat walleyes, left tied to a shoreline bush at the landing.

Did these anglers plan to return tonight? Were they leaving the fish until tomorrow? Had they simply forgotten them?

All we knew was that they wouldn't give us a straight answer if we asked them. And that they hadn't caught them in Clear Lake.

A canoe can be a camp table as well as a wilderness vehicle.

Journal Entry: Boundary Waters Canoe Area Canoe Camping Adventure

Tim Lesmeister and **Bill Slaughter** do their shtick like a smiling drill sergeant and grunt recruit.

"Where do you live?" Lesmeister asks the **Boundary Waters Canoe Area** Wilderness (BWCA) guide, midway through packing for a weekend outing in Slaughter's Ely, Minnesota, driveway.

"Ely!" comes the response.

"Where have you always lived?"

"Ely!"

"What do we eat when we go canoeing?"

"Real food!"

Lesmeister and Slaughter have made their point. Slaughter will guide us into the million-plus-acre BWCA.

We'll relax and fish and paddle when we want. We'll eat real food. A couple of hours later, we load canoes until they bulge with camp packs, food packs, coolers, camping gear, and, in Slaughter's canoe, a dog named Balls that the guide says bear-proofs his camp. Black bears have learned that BWCA campsites offer food. Campers here, like those in wilderness settings everywhere, are told to hoist their food packs, containing all their munchies, at least 10 feet off the ground, 6 feet from the closest tree trunk, and 4 feet from the nearest branch. Bears can't reach them then. Hang the pack every night, and whenever you'll be away from the camp.

Slaughter takes Balls instead. A lurking bear draws the big, black, mixed-breed dog's growls, which sends the bear back into the brush.

Campers here seldom see wolves and only sometimes see a bear. Loons, though, are visible on almost every lake and audible from almost everywhere.

Californian Tom Stienstra and I spend one entire day poking around this land of loons. We explore connected lakes and rivers, casting spinnerbaits, minnow plugs, and flies, and having a ball with feisty pike we return to the water to fight again.

Most of our party's fishing is done near the center of the lake on which we camp. Mahogany-color waters provide walleyes. The BWCA is also known for its smallmouth bass, northern pike, and lake trout. The area is rich, too, in mosquitoes and black flies.

The shore is lined with broken slabs of granite, and it's not difficult to find pieces formed perfectly to provide a comfortable perch, backrest included, from which to watch a loon guard a nesting island or to scratch a few lines in a journal. Campmates a few dozen yards away converse in muffled laughter fueled by coffee, bacon, scrambled eggs, doughnuts and rolls: real food.

This rock is encrusted with lichen, blanketed in pine needles. Where a bit of topsoil has collected or formed, new generations of trees or other plants are afoot.

Entry to the BWCA Wilderness is by permit only, to control the number of people in it and to maintain a wilderness experience.

Each year more than 200,000 people visit the BWCA. Ontario's **Quetico Provincial Park**, which adjoins it along the international border, is also a permit-only wilderness.

Permits to enter the BWCA are available for overnight and day use, and for paddle, motor, and foot travel.

Reservations, which cost $9 each, may be requested beginning December 1; phone reservations can be made beginning February 1.

Relaxing a day's end on a canoe camp outing.

Products/Services

Cabela's Foul Weather Bags ($29–$69) are made of extra-heavy-duty nylon-reinforced PVC for 100-percent waterproofing even in rugged use. A backpack features padded shoulder straps and 3,600 square inches of storage. Two duffel bags have two-way zipper tops covered by a full-length hook-and-loop splash guard.

Camp Trails' Canoe Pak ($119) was designed by outfitters as a practical bag that's easy to load and to carry across portages. Padded shoulder straps and removable hip belt aid the canoe camper. The Tripper ($149) is a larger, updated version of the Canoe Pak, and features more complete suspension and additional compression straps. It holds an impressive 8,880 cubic inches.

Canadian Waters, based in Ely, Minnesota at the doorstep of the Boundary Waters Canoe Area (U.S.) and Quetico Provincial Park (Canada) wilderness areas, bills itself "North America's Only World Class Canoe Trip Outfitter." I've paddled with Canadian Waters, and I believe them.

The company offers a wide range of trips, guided

Cabela's Foul Weather bags

(courtesy Cabela's)

and unguided, paddle-in only and fly-in, and with different gear levels. As in all camping gear, the smallest and lightest gear is the most expensive, and outfitting rates reflect that.

The firm provides even the seasoned wilderness traveler with the confidence that everything needed is aboard, and that it's tough enough to stand up to wilderness use. Even more important, outfitters provide their intimate knowledge of the area.

Canadian Waters uses Old Town canoes, including some Kevlar models. Expedition-caliber tents are

Paddling into a canoe wilderness

made to company specifications by several top firms, and sleeping bags are matched to the environment. Freeze-dried foods are the best available.

Its brochure includes some sample routes, helpfully rated separately for fishing, scenery, wildlife, challenge, and travel.

In addition to canoe trips, Canadian Waters offers motorboat trips and kayak outings, and sells new and used wilderness equipment and supplies through its retail store in downtown Ely.

Duluth Tent & Awning has been building Original Duluth Packs for more than eighty-five years and is still using the same materials and construction that made these packs famous for their ability to pack well in a canoe and comfortably carry big loads of gear across the North Country's portages.

Original Heavy Duty Duluth Packs ($79–$94) are made with 18-ounce olive drab canvas a double bottom, and 1-inch-wide flap straps. All feature an interior map pocket, hand-hammered copper rivets, and leather reinforcement at stress points. Original Duluth Packs ($69–$94) are similar but are made of 15-ounce canvas and have ¾-inch straps.

Duluth Tent & Awning's line also includes a variety of specialty canoe packs, cruiser packs, woolen clothing, pack baskets, and other canoeing equipment.

Eagle Creek offers several waterproof storage items in its amphibious travel accessories line. The new Hydro Safe Pouch measures 5¾ by 8 inches and is a basic watertight pouch to keep valuables dry. It can be worn around the neck by its strap.

The Eagle Creek Tadpole Neck Pouch has a waterproof compartment with watertight closure, two additional flap closures, a mesh pocket, and a key keeper. The Salamander and Bullfrog are waterproof fanny packs; both have mesh drain compartments as well as waterproof compartments.

Granite Gear canoe packs include Traditional Packs, using the age-old portage pack design but with a packsack made of extremely durable 1,000-denier Cordura fabric. Features include hot-cut nylon webbing, bar-tacked stress areas, and double bottoms.

The Superior One, Quetico, and Solo expedition packs offer anatomically designed harness systems, foam-padded back panels, and compression straps along the sides to stabilize the load and lash on extra gear. They're built of 1,000-denier Cordura and 1,050-denier Ballistics cloth. The Superior One is the largest, with a massive capacity of 7,400 cubic inches.

The Traveler Chest Pack is designed to hold the stuff you might need in a hurry. It attaches to D-rings on the shoulder straps of the Expedition Series packs.

Granite Gear also makes map cases, thwart bags, canoe-seat packs, and bow bags to keep a canoe camper's gear protected, organized, and available.

Sources

Boundary Waters Canoe Area information
Forest Supervisor
Superior National Forest
P.O. Box 338
Duluth, MN 55801
(218) 720–5324

**Boundary Waters Canoe Area
  Reservation Service**
P.O. Box 450
Cumberland, MD 21501
(800) 745–3399
Fax: (301) 722–9808

Cabela's
Department 9BA–50M
Sidney, NE 69160
(800) 331–3454

Camp Trails
Johnson Worldwide Associates
Camping Division
1326 Willow Road
Sturtevant, WI 53177
(800) 848–3673
Fax: (414) 884–1703
E-mail: camping@racine.jwa.com

Canadian Waters
111 East Sheridan Street
Ely, MN 55731–1299
(800) 255–2922

Duluth Tent & Awning, Inc.
P.O. Box 16024
Duluth, MN 55816–0024
(800) 777–4439

Eagle Creek
1740 LaCosta Meadows Drive
San Marcos, CA 92126–5106
(619) 471–7600
Fax: (619) 471–2536

Granite Gear
P.O. Box 278 Industrial Park
Two Harbors, MN 55616
(218) 834–6157
Fax: (218) 834–5545

Quetico Provincial Park
District Manager, Ministry of
  Natural Resources
Atikokan, Ontario POT 1CO Canada
(807) 597–2735

Bill Slaughter's Northwoods Guiding Service
2237 Grant McMahan Boulevard
Ely, MN 55731
(218) 365–2650

Chapter 13
Bicycle Camping

Bikes and RVs mix in many camping locations—here, Yellowstone National Park.

Bicycles and camping seem to go together. A few people use their bikes to get them to camping spots, although most arrange for support vehicles, cars and trucks, to carry their tents, sleeping bags, food, and spare parts. You can, however, carry your camping gear on a bicycle.

Even more popular, though, is the bicycle in the campground; the bike as a way of getting around and enjoying nature and exercise when the tent's been pitched or the RV parked.

The offerings of the companies that make bikes will not be examined here. The biking world is a highly technical one that calls for its own source-book. Count on your local bike shop and knowledgeable friends to steer you. Where camping and biking interface is what will be discussed here.

Mountain bikes—multi-geared machines with big high-flotation tires and rugged frames—are seen in many places besides mountains, and they've been cross-bred with other designs to create what some call the city bike.

The broad category called "mountain bikes" has seen a ten-fold sales increase in eight years, and today's bike is easier to ride than a multi-speed bike has ever been.

In some areas, according to the experts at bike manufacturer Shimano, about 90 percent of the bikes in use are mountain bikes. Today's mountain bikes make shifting a breeze. Cantilever brakes are sure, and fat tires take the abuse of bumps so you don't have to.

Products/Services

B.O.B. Trailers' Yak Trailer ($230) offers a low center of gravity and light weight. It carries camping and backpacking equipment on rough trails, follows the bike easily on narrow roads, and does workday duty on commutes. It is rated to hold

large main compartment that comes with a sling strap so it can be detached and used as a daypack, left and right bags with a main compartment, large rear compartment, and map/document pouch. A Rear Rack for the Tourer Pannier ($24) is also available. A Handlebar Map Pouch ($34) holds plenty of gear in the main bag, while displaying a map in a plastic-top map pouch.

Shimano says that shoes specially designed for bicycling can make pedaling more pleasant. The company, which makes a full line of biking shoes, says the shoe stabilizes the foot on the pedal, so its pedaling force is spread more evenly, and your pedaling effort is more comfortable and productive.

Some bikes and shoes work with a clip system, in which you slide your foot into a retainer. Shimano's Pedaling Dynamics (SPD) system secures the shoe to the pedal without a clip and releases it

Yak bicycle trailer by B.O.B. Trailers

(courtesy B.O.B. Trailers)

Yak bicycle trailer in action

(courtesy B.O.B. Trailers)

up to 70 pounds. The single-wheel trailer weighs just 12 pounds, and attaches at the rear-wheel hub. It mounts to mountain, cross, road, tandem, and recumbent bikes.

B-West Outdoor Specialties offers its Back-Packer line of cycling bags for the camping biker. A Front Tourer Pannier ($119) consists of two panniers each offering large compartments and a front flat pouch, and compression straps. A Front Rack for the Tourer Pannier ($24) is also available.

B-West's Rear Tourer Pannier ($189) has a

with a twist.

Bike shoes come designed for many biking varieties, from off-road racing and cycling to road and sport racing to sport recreation. Shimano's SPD C-series, designed for recreational, touring, and commuting cycling, are also made to provide comfortable walking.

In its off-road line, Shimano offers a hiking-style off-road shoe to provide more ankle protection and walking support. For leisure biking and walking, Shimano even offers an SPD sport sandal.

TLC for Your Bike

By Shimano

It used to be that when it was time for a bike ride, you just jumped aboard and away you went, peddling happily down the street. While this is still so for many cycling enthusiasts, things have changed with the advent of the mountain bike. Designed for use on all types of terrain, there's some preparation needed before you jump aboard and peddle away.

Chances are, you'll meet up with hard dirt, rocky trails, and soft sand on the same trip. It's important to be prepared, and that means starting with a thorough inspection of your equipment.

A periodic tune-up at a local bike shop is usually worth the $20 to $100 at the beginning of the season. "Having your bike in optimum working order is just as important as having a map," according to Robert Plunkett, technical service manager at Shimano, a leading manufacturer of bicycle components. "Having a chain come off at the wrong time is one of the most frustrating experiences a cyclist can have."

To keep that from happening, have your local bike shop check the front and rear derailleurs to make sure they move the chain from one chain-wheel to the next when changing gears. If needed, the shop will lightly lubricate the chain and pivot points on the derailleurs.

As part of the tune-up, the bike shop will set the proper tension on the brakes, which provide stopping power on both front and rear wheels. They'll also adjust the brake pads so they are hitting properly on each side of the rims and not rubbing the tires.

Along with the work done on your bike at the shop, there are certain checklist items you can do and should do yourself each time you head for the open road.

As for the tires themselves, make sure they are properly inflated. And learn how to fix a flat before you go! Practice taking the wheel on and off, and carry a spare tube just in case.

Besides the extra tube, Shimano's Plunkett advises carrying the proper trail tools. A multi-function tool that includes sockets, spoke wrench, and chain tool fits the bill nicely. Add an air pump, patch kit, filled water bottle, and some high-energy foods.

Now that the bike pack is outfitted, make sure you are, too. Lip balm and sunscreen are absolute musts, as is an approved bicycle helmet.

Those funky nylon shorts and tights are something besides a fashion statement. They fit the bent-leg cycling position, and special seaming and padding provide ultimate comfort. Good cycling footwear increases stamina and reduces fatigue. Some companies even offer a shoe-and-pedal system for better performance.

All set to go? To determine the route and the amount of time it takes, take a map so you can plan accordingly. Don't forget to tell someone where you're going and when you should be back.

With these precautions, you'll protect the investment you have in your mountain bike and enjoy the ride that much more.

Chapter 14
Water Sports

Many people camp to be near the water—for swimming, fishing, boating, sailing, nature study and more.

Fishing Basics

By Elizabeth May Griffin (Age 9)
as told to Steven A. Griffin

It's fun to catch fish, and you can take time to swim or watch birds. Fishing places are often nice places to visit. And fishing is easy.

You need to know a few things.

Campers ready their fishing gear.

You need to know how big fish should be to keep. Different kinds of fish need to be different lengths. You need to be able to measure fish, and tell what kind you have.

People can teach you the different kinds of fish, and you can read about them. There's really no other way. Well, you can guess. But you might be wrong. And then you might get into trouble.

Some tackle boxes have rulers on them, but they might not be long enough for some fish, such as a big rainbow trout. So you need a ruler or tape.

Sometimes there are special rules for fishing on certain rivers or lakes. You need to read the rule book.

To start catching fish: you don't need a fish pole. You really just need a stick with a hook, sinker, line.

Basic Gear

A hook is a wire bent into a J-shape. It has a loop at the top to tie the fishing line to. The box that fishing line comes in usually shows easy knots to use. The hook holds the bait, and it holds the fish if one bites.

Line is what we call the string we use to fish with. Some is clear, and some is not. Thick line is usually stronger, but sometimes fish see it and won't bite.

A sinker is a piece of heavy stuff you use to hold the bait down. Most sinkers are made of lead, but new ones are made of other materials. People

For many campers, fishing is part of the winning mix.

think lead sinkers can cause problems for birds.

That's all you really need for fishing. But a fishing pole makes it more fun.

I use Mom's fishing pole. The reel has a push button. You push it down and hold it. When you let the button up, the line can come out. When you turn the handle, the line can't come out anymore, and it comes in as you turn the crank.

(courtesy Columbia Sportswear)

Fishing is a natural activity for the camper.

Tactics and Tricks

The easiest fishing is straight down. You don't have to cast. If you cast way out, you can't see the fish and it drives you nuts, because you don't think there are any down there. If you can see them, even if they don't bite, at least you know they're there. That's what makes piers and docks so popular. You can drop your hook into the water, and sometimes you can see the fish.

If you have to cast, first look behind you and make sure there's nobody there who could get hooked. If you're using a *spincast* reel, push the button down with your thumb. With a *spinning* reel flip over the bail, or wire loop, and hold the line down with your finger. Swing the rod backward until it points back over your shoulder. Then whip it forward and let go of the line or the button. The bait or lure will fly through the air (with the greatest of ease) and pull the line with it.

Bait Basics

Bait works better than lures to start with, because lures aren't real. Lures are made of metal

or plastic, or wood, or feathers, and they're supposed to look like something good to eat. But bait is something good to eat. You can let bait sit there, too. You have to reel a lure in.

All kinds of things can be used for bait. Even hot dogs work for some fish. Night crawlers work for most of them. Worms work, too. Really, fish seem to like crawlers better, but I like worms because they're not as big and disgusting. Minnows are good, too. So are wax worms and grubs. Some people fish with corn. Stinking rotten catfish blood junk works for catfish. It's stinky and disgusting. Not to a catfish, though.

Bites

Wait and wait for a bite. The bobber will wiggle, or the line will tug. Reel the fish in, measure it, and see if it's long enough. Take it home if it's big enough, clean it and eat it.

Sometimes, even if a fish is big enough, we decide to throw it back. Maybe we don't like eating that kind of fish. Maybe we don't have the place or stuff to cook it. Maybe we just don't want to keep fish that day. It's still fun to catch them.

Bobbers help you catch fish. They float. They keep the bait off the bottom, so the fish can see it and get it. They also tell you when a fish bites. When a fish bites it will bob under and come up. Sometimes it will come up, anyway. Sometimes it stays under until the fish lets go. When the bobber bobs, reel it in. You can give the line a tug first to make sure the fish is on. Sometimes it seems as the fish flies off when you give it a tug.

Landing Catches

Little fish can be cranked right in. A big fish pulls so hard that sometimes line comes out of the reel with a rattley sound. That's the drag, which helps tire the fish out. There's no use trying to crank it in while it's pulling out line. When it stops, reel in as much line as you can.

When you get the fish near shore or the dock or near the boat, you can pick it up if it's small. If it's big, it helps to have a net to scoop it up.

Tackle Box Exam

You don't need a tackle box to go fishing, but they're nice and handy to keep things in. Here's what was in my tackle box the day we wrote this story:

- Stick bobbers and round bobbers, plus a few little ice fishing bobbers. I like round bobbers best.
- Rubber fish eggs for bait. They stink. Keep the package closed. Trout like them.
- Little rubber grubs called Mr. Twisters. Their tales wiggle, and bass and walleyes like them. I caught something on yellow ones, but I forget what.
- Little spinner lures. The blade spins when you cast and reel it right in. Trout and panfish and other fish like them.
- Spinning frog lure. The front half stays put, but the back half, with the legs, spins when you reel it it. I haven't caught a fish with it, but it's fun to cast it out and watch it spin.
- Eagle Claw "Good Luck" hooks. They would come in handy if all my hooks were gone. They would be good luck then.
- Disgusting year-old marshmallows. Pink, purple, and orange. Bluegills sometimes nibble them off the hook.
- A litter bag, so you don't make a mess of your favorite fishing spot.
- One of my favorites, a Mr. Twister worm that I caught with my line. Sometimes lures catch fish. Sometimes you can even

catch a *lure*. I have a bunch of bobbers, all different sizes, I caught or fished out of the water with my hands. One is covered with dried weeds.
- Clippers for snipping line.
- A bubble gum wrapper. It's Rainbow Blow. It comes in rainbow colors.
- Fish hooks. Little sharp ones and the best kind.
- A weird gizmo, oh, that's two spinners hooked together.
- A lead-headed jig that looks like the cat ate it. That reminds me, it's good to keep hooks and lures where little kids and animals can't mess with them.
- A good luck hook I caught.
- A Snoopy bobber that doesn't work anymore. It used to lie on its back. When a fish would bite, it stood straight up.
- Sinkers. You need different kinds and different sizes. Little ones for bluegills and small baits. Big ones to cast a long ways and hold down frisky minnows.

There are other things you need. You need a ruler. You should have sunscreen and bug stuff. Bugs seem to hang out with fish.

That's really all you need to know about fishing. Now, go fishing and have fun!!

Sailing: Riding the Wind

If you feel a call to go sailing, you might be feeling an urge centuries-old, aided today by high-tech materials and design.

The first boats were logs placed in the water. Several logs combined made a stabler craft. Finally early sailors returned to single-log designs, but hollowed out and outfitted them with a magnificent creation: the sail.

The sail harnessed the power of the wind; the seemingly magical movement of air inspired by the sun. The first sailors, then, were pioneers not only in movement on water, but in the use of solar power!

It's worth noting, though, that the first sailboats also used muscle power on oars along with sails. On some days, when the wind falls, that still happens!

Some call the sail one of the greatest inventions in history, making possible safer transportation of many people and much cargo, where before only small boats could go.

Sailing for most people today is a hobby, and a popular one.

Popular Hobby

The National Marine Manufacturers Association reports that almost 1.3 million sailboats were in use in the United States in one recent year—and that didn't even include the boats at opposite ends of the sailing spectrum—those big boats using inboard motors for auxiliary power, and the sailboards that have exploded in popularity in the past few years. Sailing claimed almost 8 percent of the nation's recreational fleet.

Experts offer several reasons for the ever-increasing number of people who love to sail. A big one is that many smaller sailboats can be carried on car-top racks or small trailers. Another is that sailing schools make it easy to learn the fundamentals of this sport safely and enjoyably.

Sailing can be pleasantly simple or incredibly intricate. Many seasoned sailors, some at the top of the racing game, describe childhood voyages on tiny simple craft that left them sailors for life. A good starting boat is the small cat-rigged boat, with single mast and single sail.

Sailing Small

Small sailboats often feature centerboards or daggerboards to provide stability. Larger boats have keels to accomplish the same thing, with hun-

dreds of pounds of weight sometimes added to secure the boat in the water. Keels offer wonderful stability, but these boats must be hoisted, not pulled, onto a trailer, can't handle really shallow waters, and are best in situations where they can be moored or slipped.

Daggerboards and centerboards reach into the water through a well or slot in the center of the boat. A centerboard pivots to extend farther. A daggerboard is simply raised and lowered vertically.

The cat-rigged boat has a single sail. A sloop-rigged craft has the mainsail, billowing behind the mast, and a jib attached to the mainstay or front cable from the bow to the mast. A schooner carries three sails. Any might have a spinnaker, a special sail for catching the wind from behind.

Wind Words

One often thinks of two kinds of sailing: with the wind, and against it.

Obviously, sailing with the wind is easiest. The wind fills the sails and presses the boat along on its path, which can be adjusted with the rudder.

Sailing into the wind is enchantingly more complex. Sails are adjusted so that the air gives them their curve. The air then travels across them as if they were a vertical wing; the air moving faster on the outside of the curve creates lower pressure, and the boat is pulled in that direction. The keel or centerboard counteracts this movement, and the boat squirts forward, as close as 45 degrees to the wind.

It's the constant attention paid the wind, and the constant and ever-changing combination of sail, angle, rudder and more that make sailing such a beguilingly challenging art.

New Sailor's Glossary

hull: the shell of the boat in which the crew rides

keel: extension of hull several feet into water; does work of centerboard in larger sailboats

centerboard: board used to stabilize small sailboat, pivots to raise and lower

daggerboard: removable centerboard used in some small sailboats

mast: central post on a sailboat that supports the mainsail

boom: beam attached to the mast that provides bottom edge of mainsail

stays: cables that hold the mast upright

rudder: paddle-shape plate that directs the boat through the water

tiller: handle on smaller sailboats that turns the rudder and thus steers the boat

cat-rigged: single sail

sloop-rigged: two-sailed boat

mainsail: triangular sail supported by and extending back from the mast

jib: triangular sail attached to mainstay or front cable

spinnaker: special sail for sailing with the wind

cleat: metal fitting to which ropes (lines) are tied

lines: ropes on a boat

mooring: tying a boat in a position at dock or slip

slip: "parking spot" for a boat in the water at a marina

running: sailing with the wind (southward, for example, powered by a north wind)

reaching: sailing across the wind (westward, for example, powered by a north wind)

beating: sailing into the wind (northwestward, for example, into a north wind)

heeling: the boat's leaning caused by the wind; it is counteracted by the boat's crew leaning in the opposite direction.

leeway: sideways movement of the boat; it is counteracted by the centerboard or keel

luff: the shaking of a sail improperly tensioned (when, for example, facing into the wind)

tacking: zigzagging to move upwind

Journal Entry: Navigable Nature—Aboard the *Sea Princess*

Kathie Petrie moves through the nature excursion boat *Sea Princess,* handing each person a laminated chart showing several of the seabirds and raptors they're likely—and hoping—to see in the area.

They're welcome aboard the *Sea Princess.* Her Islesford Historical Cruise is one of literally dozens sprinkled around Acadia National Park on the "Downeast" Maine seacoast. This tour stays nearshore, within a band of islands that keeps seas mild. Petrie is in her seventh year as a seasonal ranger with the National Park Service, and as part of her job she serves as interpreter on this cruise out of Northeast Harbor on Mount Desert Island. Several of her passengers are staying in a campground just a few minutes' drive away.

Nature touring, outings blending adventure with education, is becoming popular everywhere. Here at Acadia whale-watching excursions set out from Bar Harbor and several other ports. A guided lobster boat cruise offers close-up views of seals, plus a chance to haul a lobster trap aboard and chat with a lobsterman. Some boats even feature live-action video provided by divers beneath the boat. Sailing ships, including windjammers, offer cruises lasting a few hours or a few days. Some outings feature their own staff naturalists to offer interpretation; National Park Service rangers such as Petrie accompany and interpret many cruises.

The town of Northeast Harbor, Petrie explains, sits on the shore of what's called "The Great Harbor," a large, protected bay with two deepwater inlets. It proved popular and profitable in the 1800s and early 1900s, when ships came here to trade. Many ships

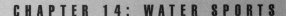

launched here, too. Maine offered plenty of what shipbuilders needed: quality timber, and deep inlets into which boats could be set afloat once built. Thirty-five shipbuilders continue the craft on Mount Desert Island, says Petrie. Each year they launch vessels from rowboats to yachts.

Early in the almost-three-hour-long voyage, the boat slows and Petrie calls the passengers' attention to a huge pile of large sticks on a high rock. It's a nest, a huge one, and atop it sits an osprey. The bird flaps its wings and rises to a slightly higher lookout, but doesn't seem afraid. This is a regular stop for the *Sea Princess,* and the osprey has apparently grown accustomed to seeing the boat and its passengers.

The boat motors on past Sutton's Island and its osprey. Petrie says Europeans in the early 1700s reportedly bought this island from Native Americans for 1½ quarts of rum. It's doubtful both parties had the same understanding of the sale, says Petrie.

Natural forces left their marks on the island, too. From the boat Petrie points out a large white boulder, alone near the top of a mountain. "That was brought here and dropped off by the last glacier," the force that carved out most of this coastline region.

A navigation marker, the first of its kind in these waters and okayed by Congress in 1804, bears a sentry: A mature bald eagle surveys the waters nearby for a meal.

On another rocky island a herd of harbor seals sun themselves.

Most coastline boat traffic now is either pleasure oriented or focused on fishing, especially lobstering. Trap markers bob in most inshore waters. The *Sea Princess* threads her way through them on her way to this cruise's port of call, Islesford village on Little Cranberry Island. It's one of five islands making up one governmental unit, the Town of Cranberry.

On Little Cranberry Island stand several old buildings. One was once a ship's store, whose dock reached waters deep enough to welcome a schooner. Upstairs had been a sail shop. Trade involved ice, cobblestones, smoked fish, fresh fish and other supplies. Round cobblestones for street-building, Petrie says, fetched thirty cents a ton in Boston. That was profitable somehow, even after they were handled several times: collected on the island and brought to the dock, then loaded onto the ship, and finally unloaded at Boston Harbor.

Petrie interrupts herself to point out a guillemot, a bird she describes as a relative of the now-extinct great auk and the recovering common puffin, also seen in Maine's waters. Of Maine's 3,000 coastal islands, about 350 support nesting seabirds, waterfowl, and wading birds. Besides guillemots and puffins, seabirds include herring, black-backed and laughing gulls; least, Arctic, common and roseate terns; Leach's petrel and double-crested cormorant. Common eider headline waterfowl, and wading birds include herons, egrets, and ibises. It's a birder's dream.

Personal Watercraft

They're flashy and fast and fun. Used incorrectly illegally or discourteously, they make other boaters and lake users furious. They're boats, in form and function, and they're claiming their place on the water. They're personal watercraft (PWC), sometimes known by the brand names Jet Skis or WaveRunners.

PWC are small, inboard-powered boats equipped with water-jet propulsion and made for one, two, or even three people. They've hit a responsive chord in a legion of watersport fans, and struck a harsh discord in others.

Bad PR

If a class of transportation could hire a public relations representative, PWC probably would. The sporty little craft, so popular with their users, are so, well, unpopular with others. And the PR person's challenge would be to distinguish between the watercraft and some of their drivers.

The conflict, you see, is not so much between *uses* as *users*. It's less about *boats* than *boaters*. It's often a matter of manners.

Conflict seems a growing problem. As PWC numbers continue to grow, so do refinements in the craft themselves. Advances in design, engines, jet thrusters, and plastics have placed increasingly better craft on the water.

PWC Types

PWC are available in stand-up and sit-down models. Most consider the stand-ups the best performers, the sports cars of the class. For maximum maneuverability, they're probably your craft. For comfort on a long day afloat, though, sit-down PWC get the nod. PWC were first designed as one-person craft. Drivers wanted to share the fun, however, and soon two-person machines were available and then three-person.

An entire after-market industry niche has emerged: trailers, lifts, clothing, and other accessories, all geared to the PWC and its operator.

All that design and engineering, all that fun, and still there are problems. People don't always get along. PWC users just seem to rub some other boaters the wrong way.

PWC Principles

A big part of the solution to friction between user groups is safer and more considerate operation of PWC. You can cut the problems by following these tips as you enjoy your craft, according to the National Marine Manufacturers Association and others.

- Learn and follow all the rules that apply to power boating.
- Many states have laws requiring PWC to stay a minimum distance away from any other vessel, except another PWC, and specified distances from any dock, raft, or swimming area. Obey them.
- Make sure you know your watercraft and its operation before going afloat. Read all the manufacturer's recommendations. Then go slow as you learn more in practice.
- Don't cross within 150 feet of the stern of another boat under power.
- Always wear a personal flotation device (life jacket) while operating a PWC. It's the law, and good common sense.
- Wear protective eyeglasses to keep spray from temporarily blocking your vision.
- Wear gloves and footwear for protection and positive control.
- Wear a wetsuit. Hypothermia can be dangerous even in relatively warm water.
- Watch at all times for others on the

water such as boaters, skiers, swimmers, and others. Watch for hazards such as stumps and docks, too.

- Don't operate your PWC under the influence of drugs or alcohol, and don't smoke on or near it. Remember that a long day on the water affects judgment and reaction time much like drugs or alcohol. Take breaks, and slow down.
- Don't alter your PWC to make it louder.
- Be sure to comply with slow, no-wake rules. That means the minimum speed necessary to steer the craft. The PWC will still shoot water from the jet thruster, but movement should be minimal.
- Ride only in daylight.
- Avoid threading a path through boat crowds, or wake jumping; that's reckless driving in some law-enforcement books.

Inflatable Boats

What float big and stow small? Inflatables, and their popularity is swelling, especially with campers.

About one new boat in twenty is an inflatable, according to the National Marine Manufacturers

Association (NMMA).

Inflated Popularity

Inflatables aren't new; it's their popularity that's taken on new life. The boats themselves have been used for more than thirty years, and many of those original inflatables are still afloat.

The modern, quality inflatable boat is, like all its water-borne relatives, an investment. Prices can quickly reach $2,000 and way beyond, depending upon the size and features you require. You get a lot for your money, though.

Modern inflatables are made of tough fabrics resistant to tears or punctures. Sure it pays to use some discretion to prevent them from being dragged or scraped on rocks or rough surfaces. Inflatable boats, however, are very buoyant and stable; quality inflatable makers work to keep centers of gravity low and beams wide for stability. The goal is a buoyant, seaworthy boat, and it's met by several top-of-the-line makers. The craft normally have several air chambers so they will continue to float, even if one chamber is punctured. The smallest inflatables have at least two air chambers; the largest often have six or more.

These are big boats in small-when-deflated packages. Many can be carried easily by one person, inflated in minutes and enjoyed for years. Large air valves provide quick inflation with high-volume bellows or pump, which is often provided.

Options Available

You can buy an inflatable boat with a steering console, windshield, seats (even upholstered bucket seats!) and floorboards. Some have raised bows and motor mounts, and some can pull skiers. Speeds can reach more than 35 miles per hour. Some are even jet-powered, like personal watercraft.

There are two categories of inflatables: soft-bottomed inflatables and solid-bottom boats called rigid inflatable boats (RIB) or hard-bottom (HB)

(courtesy Zodiac of North America)

The River Renegade

inflatables. The latter generally provide better performance, but give up storage, deflated size, and weight advantages. Some now have rigid, V-bottom hulls for handling and performance. Soft-bottom boats are lighter; you have the option to add floorboards to them.

The floorboard decision depends upon the boat, its intended use, and your performance expectations. Floorboards in dinghies provide a more rigid boat and increased speed, with a slight trade-off in stowability. That drawback can be minimized with a slatted floor. Transom inflatables can be purchased with slatted floors that roll up for storage in their own stowing bags. In bigger inflatables, those designed to carry outboards of up to 55 h.p., solid floorboards may be needed to stiffen the boat under power. It's a safe bet, though, that many more inflatables are moved about by smaller outboards, those in the 3-h.p. to 4-h.p. range.

Oar Power?

Inflatables can also be powered by oar. It does take some practice to learn to row them; short, brisk rowing strokes are the rule, with some pausing time to let the boat take advantage of the stroke. Most boats come not only with oarlocks, but with stowing hardware for the oars themselves.

Inflatables Measure Up

A typical dinghy might measure 8 feet long, 4 feet wide, and weigh in at 32 pounds. Add a deck, and there's another 18 pounds. Twin air chambers provide enough buoyancy for a three-person load weighing 550 pounds, and up to a 3-horsepower outboard power on the stern.

A bigger boat might stretch almost 13 feet long and more than 5 feet across. Built to hold up to seven people totaling as much as 1,400 pounds, the boat itself weighs only 97 pounds with another 54 pounds of deck.

The solid-bottom RIB boat might be 10 feet long, just under 5 feet wide, and weigh a total of 112 pounds. You can load it with five people weighing an aggregate 925 pounds, and push it with a 10 h.p. motor. The price still comes in at just over $3,000.

Boat manufacturers offer extras such as bow-dodgers, which attach to the front of the boat to keep spray from reaching the occupants and equipment. Soft-bottomed boats can be trimmed with wooden decks, customized with extra seating, or rigged with rigid outboard-motor brackets. Storage bags attach beneath solid seats to hold gear. Boats that incorporate rigid transoms can be fitted with wheels for easy launching and landing.

That's thinking ahead. For once you discover the convenience of inflatables, it's a sure bet you'll be afloat in one often.

Boat Safely!

Safe boating is as important to the camper as to the full-time boater. These tips from the NMMA provide a good casting-off point:

- designate a skipper who hasn't been drinking alcohol and won't drink it while on duty;
- require that everyone aboard wear a personal flotation device; and
- don't exceed the boat's safe-carrying capacity or power rating.

NMMA offers a checklist, too, of boating considerations:

- is the drain plug securely in place?
- is there a personal flotation device—life jacket—aboard for each passenger?
- is the steering system working smoothly?
- is there enough fuel aboard, and not leaking fluid or fumes?
- is the battery fully charged, with clean, tight, connections?
- is the engine in neutral?
- are weather conditions safe?

- is electrical and electronic gear working?
- is emergency gear—fire extinguisher, bailer, paddle, anchor and line, signaling device, tool kit, etc.—in place?

If you're towing your boat, as many campers do,

- is the coupler, hitch, and hitch ball the same size?
- are coupler and safety chains secured to the hitch?
- are fasteners fastened?
- is the boat securely tied to the trailer? (The winch line is not a tie down)
- are wheel lug nuts tight?
- are wheel bearings adjusted and maintained?
- is the load within the capacity?
- are tires properly inflated?
- are trailer lights working?
- are trailer brakes adjusted and working?

Products/Services

American Camper offers several models of inflatable river boats, with models up to a ten-person boat with a wooden motor mount. Its boats,

certified by the NMMA, are made with strong, rubberized 420-denier nylon and offer multiple air chambers.

Crazy Creek took its Original Chair concept afloat with the Canoe Chair, specially designed to fit most canoe seats. Straps feature quick-release buckles. The Canoe Chair II has the same features as the Canoe Chair with an additional 5-inch flap for extra back comfort.

Zodiac's Camper Special inflatable is designed especially for RV owners. It inflates in less than five minutes with a fast-flow 12-volt electric inflator and deflates in seconds. The floor-board system simply rolls up with the boat and fits neatly into a compact bag for storage. Once the boat is rolled up, it fits in an RV storage compartment or the trunk of the tow vehicle.

The Camper's Special is available in 10-foot 2-inch, and 8-foot 6-inch models, and comes with electric inflator, bench seat, oars and oarlocks, and other accessories.

Zodiac has also introduced its River Renegade inflatable ($1,700), a recreational riverboat that is easy to assemble, durable, and folds down to the size of a sleeping bag. The 10-foot 6-inch boat is 4 feet 11-inches wide with a tube diameter of 16 inches. It weights just 50 pounds. In can be inflated in less than five minutes with a foot pump. An optional rowing frame can be added.

Sources

American Camper
Nelson/Weather-Rite
P.O. Box 14488
Lenexa, KS 66285–4488
(913) 492–3200
Fax: (913) 492–8749

Crazy Creek Products
P.O. Box 1050
1401 South Broadway
Red Lodge, MT 59068
(406) 446–3446
Fax: (406) 446–1411

Zodiac of North America
P.O. Box 400
Stevensville, MD 21666
(410) 643–4141
Fax: (410) 643–4491

Chapter 15
Getting Your Bearings

There are some pieces of equipment that are almost automatically associated with camping: tent, Dutch oven, map, and compass. The first two are discussed elsewhere in this book. The map and compass have found their way here, as have exciting new tools that electronically do the work of a map and compass.

Maps and compasses do similar things. They help us figure out where we are in relation to the rest of the world. Either of them alone is a big help in the wild, but they're more valuable when used together than individually.

A map, at its simplest, is a drawing of what our surroundings look like. At its most complex, it is a computer-generated storehouse of information on the land and what stands on it. A compass is as simple as a magnetized bit of metal that aligns itself with the natural magnetism of the Earth. It can be a survey-quality precision instrument, too.

Both map and compass depend on the ability of the user to understand and manipulate the information they offer.

Maps

If you're camping in a national, provincial, state, or county park, chances are the park will offer you a map of the area. These are typically simple and have major landmarks and areas of

interest noted. The map will have an arrow showing north, so that you *orient* it to your compass (more on that in a minute).

Larger, wilder areas often call for a *topographic* map, which show elevation and relief: hills, valleys, and other changes in the surface that are distinctive landmarks as well as obstacles to overcome and avoid. For information on topographic maps for your area, contact the U.S. Geological Survey Map Sales office.

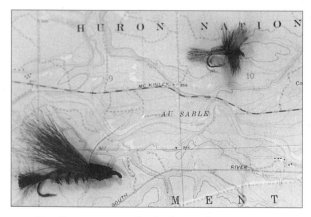

Reading a map can be the key to fine camping sites.

Details, Details

The amount of detail a map offers depends on how much area it represents. Most topographic maps are 7.5-minute or 15-minute series. The larger the number, the larger the area shown, and the less detail contained. That designation usually appears in the upper right hand corner of the map. "Minutes" confuses some people. Scale is a little easier to understand. A map is a smaller representation of a big area. Each inch on the map represents a larger distance in life. In one common topographic scale, one inch on the map equals 24,000 inches in real life. In another, the ratio is 1:62,500. The bigger number means less detail. The scale is noted at the bottom center of the map.

Topographic maps have *contour lines*. Depending on the map, each of these lines represents a change in elevation of a certain distance. The land is higher or lower than the area next to it. The map advises you how much change, in feet or meters, each line describes. This distance is called the *interval*. The closer these interval lines appear on the map, the steeper the hill or valley.

Topographic and other maps will also offer a *legend*, a guide to the symbols that represent roads, trails, rivers, buildings, quarries, and other features. Study it before you set out.

The Big Picture

Where in the world are you? Your map is one small chunk of the globe, and its location on Earth is described in longitude and latitude. Latitude lines are a system of circles drawn around the Earth parallel to the equator. There are 90 degrees of *north latitude* above the equator; 90 below it. Longitude is a series of circles drawn around the Earth perpendicular to the equator, through the North and South Poles. There are 360 degrees of longitude, with 0 placed arbitrarily through Greenwich, England. You'll find the latitude and longitude measurements along the edges of your topographic map.

Compass Connection

Moving from map to compass, the map bears an arrow or other symbol showing the direction north.

It also tells of *declination*. The Earth's magnetic field does not run exactly north and south. So a map drafted along the lines of true north and south does not match the magnetic world. The difference is declination, and the amount of it varies—from minor to considerable—depending on your location. In some areas careful compass work over a long distance, not paying attention to declination, won't get you to your goal.

Compass Types

There are several types of compasses available. Most are filled with a liquid that helps the needle settle down quickly and makes *orienteering*, or finding your way by compass, much simpler. The needle will always point to magnetic north when the compass is held flat, unless there's another strong magnetic force nearby.

Pocket compasses are handy for checking on

Brunton Sportsman's Choice compass series

(courtesy The Brunton Company)

directions so you can reverse them to find your way back out of wild country.

Get Oriented

An orienteering compass can be used in conjunction with a map. It has a plastic *base* and can be set on a map so that the map's information can be viewed through the compass base. On the base is an arrow called the *sighting line* that runs parallel with the long edge of the base. Mounted on the base is a round dial called the *housing,* which contains the magnetic *needle* within a fluid. The housing also features an *orienting arrow* that turns when the housing dial is turned.

To determine a compass bearing from a map, align the north arrow on the compass housing (not the magnetic needle) with the course you want to take, then the edge of the compass base with the magnetic north lines on the map. You're not using the compass' magnetic qualities now, just its protractor features. You can read the bearing you wish to take from the compass's pointer.

To follow that course in the field, make sure the bearing remains at the compass pointer, and align the compass so that the red end of the needle lines up with the north arrow in the compass housing. Sight along the edge of the compass and locate a landmark in the distance. Walk to it, then repeat the process and locate another landmark.

Field Work

To take a bearing in the field, hold the compass with the sighting line pointed to the destination. Without moving the sighting line, turn the dial until the north arrow on the housing and the north end of the magnetic needle line up. You can read the bearing in degrees at the sighting line.

To blend the map and compass for a better understanding of the terrain you're looking at, *orient* your map by aligning the map's magnetic north lines with the red north arrow on the compass.

Check the declination in the area you're visiting. If it's more than a few degrees, and declination lines aren't drawn on the map, you'll want to draw some yourself. Some compasses can be adjusted for the declination so you don't have to keep it in mind until you readjust it when visiting another area.

GPS: Advice from the Skies

The Global Positioning System—often referred to by its acronym GPS—is a U.S. government-managed system of satellites which orbit Earth twice a day while transmitting information on the exact time,

and their latitude, longitude, and altitude positions.

In all there are twenty-four satellites circling Earth about 12,000 miles up, providing around-the-clock service anywhere on the globe.

Your receiver needs to receive the transmission of at least three satellites, and then it computes your precise location. With reception of four signals, some units also compute altitude.

GPS was originally developed to serve U.S. military needs. Its value has broadened, though, to many civilian uses and users; not the least of whom is the camper, boater, and backcountry traveler who wants to know where he or she is.

Your GPS receiver processes the satellites'

Magellan GPS receivers

(courtesy Magellan)

information to either provide you with an exact latitude/longitude location or to sketch it on a plotter or map.

Ways They Work

Different GPS units work in different ways. All count on signals from several satellites. Most use signals from five satellites. Some units process each signal, one after the other in a series. Others feature parallel processing and compute data from all five satellites at the same time for the quickest possible positioning.

Accuracy

Standard civilian GPS reception is accurate to within 25 yards. A military signal system is much more precise. To avoid giving a potential enemy too much edge, the government sometimes intentionally injects Selective Availability interference, reducing accuracy to within about 110 yards.

The GPS user, though, can use a technique called differential GPS (DGPS) to overcome that interference and boost overall accuracy. A GPS receiver is placed at a known location, and position information from it used to calculate a correction factor, which is then transmitted to other GPS receivers in the area. The resulting practical accuracy is to within about 10 yards.

Where GPS technology comes in handiest is when a number of these locations are connected: when you take a reading, store it in memory, then add another, thus sketching your path a point at a time. That makes it simple to backtrack your trail. Or you can call up any previous "waypoint" for a reading on the quickest "as the bird flies" path to it, provided you can pass through the terrain.

How popular is GPS? Industry estimates said that by 1996, about $1 billion in GPS products would have been sold, with an estimated $5 billion by the year 2000.

Products/Services

American Camper's Orienteering Map Compass features a sighting mirror, transparent base with built-in magnifying glass, and luminous pointer. The company's Map Compass is simpler, with a clear ruled base, luminous pointer, and metric and mile scales. A Watch Style Compass comes in an ABS-plastic case with cover, lanyard ring, and luminous needle. American Camper also offers a ball-type clip-on compass, and a compact compass/thermometer/whistle combination.

Brunton offers a full range of compass products, many designed specifically for camping and other outdoor recreation. Its Adventure Series map compasses ($12–$46) feature cobalt-steel needles

sealed in anti-static, permanently clear liquid. Declination can be adjusted without tools, and the azimuth ring features easy to read numbers. Various models offer gunsight, direct, and prismatic sighting systems.

Brunton also markets a twenty-five-minute-long video and compass combination, *The ABC's of Compass & Map* ($31), which covers compass types and their features, magnetism, the Earth's magnetic field and magnetic declination, the importance of a compass in the field, bearing taking, types of maps, reading maps and scales, visual and poor weather navigation, and using map and compass together.

A Brunton Trails Kit included a Trails Illustrated topo map, compass, and map case.

For more casual applications, Brunton offers its Sportsman's Choice series of accessory compasses ($4–$9), all offer a cobalt-steel needle, sealed in an anti-static, permanently clear-liquid dampening housing. Tag-along, clip-on, and pin-on compasses are included in the line.

Normark offers several compasses of interest to campers.

The Normark Wrist Compass can be read at an angle of up to 15 degree from level—handy when you're in a hurry—and is waterproof and shock resistant. The pin-on Pocket/Lapel Compass offers the same features, with a settling time of just four to five seconds, thanks to a magnet pivoting on a fine sapphire-jewel bearing.

For mirror and map reading work, the Normark Mirror Compass features a high-definition mirror, luminous scale ring, liquid-filled capsule, sapphire-jewel bearings, and non-magnetic pivot. The base has a magnifier and slip-free mounting pads.

Eagle Electronics' AccuNav Sport hand-held GPS has a five-parallel-channel receiver, with four One Touch Command Keys that provide instant access to various screens for easy use. An internal lithium back-up battery protects against information loss.

Learning to use the GPS can be a challenge. Eagle has made it easier with a ninety-minute-long

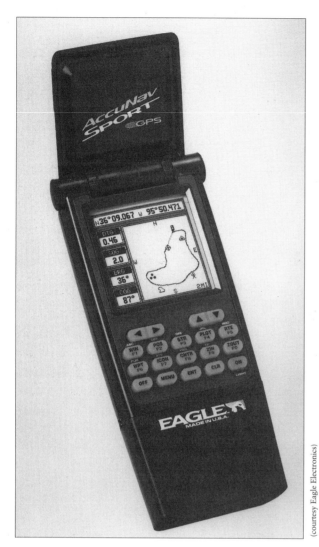

Eagle AccuNav Sport hand-held GPS unit

(courtesy Eagle Electronics)

Garmin GPS 38 Personal Navigator

(courtesy Garmin International)

instructional video, *Mark Your Spots with GPS*. The video is focused on Eagle's AccuNav Sport hand-held GPS unit. Included are instructions for saving waypoints, naming and numbering waypoints, recalling recorded waypoints, creating routes, using event markers and icons, plus other functions. The video can be purchased from any of more than 900 Eagle dealers or by calling (800) 324–0045. To learn the location of your nearest Eagle dealer call (800) 932–4534.

Garmin recently added its GPS 38 Personal Navigator to its line of GPS receivers, which include the GPS 40 and GPS 45. The GPS 38 weighs just 9 ounces, is waterproof and is DGPS ready.

The GPS 40 and GPS 45 are similar, except that the GPS 40 has an internal, self-contained antenna.

The GPS 38's enhanced operating software system includes EZinit for quick and easy first-time initialization; Backtrack to allow users to exactly retrace their route without having to create waypoints along the way; compass navigation that graphically depicts a rotating compass dial; redesigned moving map for larger presentation of navigation information; and other features.

The GPS 38, like all of Garmin's other hand-held receivers, uses the company's MultiTrac8 receiver, which tracks up to eight satellite signals simultaneously.

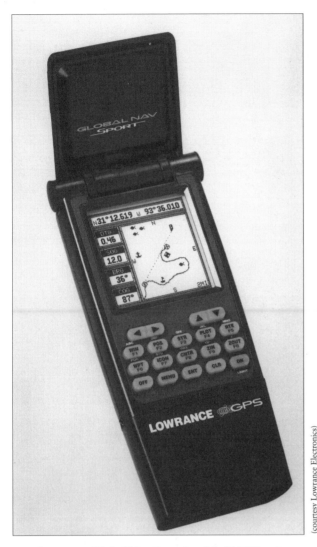

Lowrance Global Nav Sport hand-held GPS unit

Magellan GPS 4000

Lowrance's Global Map Sport hand-held GPS includes a built-in background map of the world. That's primarily for boaters. Land-based users might consider adding mini-cartridges from Lowrance's Inland Mapping System, which offers detailed mapping of the Lower 48, including the names and locations of more than 140,000 cities; 30,000 national, state, and county parks; U.S. routes and interstate highways; and waterways such as lakes, streams, and coastal waters.

You select the cartridge from the sixty-four available, and the screen displays the map, with a blinking cursor showing your position. You have more than a map; you have a picture that includes

you! Advanced mapping graphics offer plotting ranges from 1/10 to 4,000 nautical miles.

The Global Map Sport operates on standard AA batteries, rechargeable Ni-Cad batteries, or a 6- to 35-volt external power source.

Lowrance's Global Nav Sport hand-held GPS has five-parallel-channel processing, plus an internal lithium back-up battery that stores information for up to ten years. That eliminates the fear of losing information when operating batteries die and are removed.

The Global Nav Sport offers a programmable "windows" feature that lets you customize screen options to match your needs. The unit operates on AA batteries, rechargeable Ni-Cad batteries, or an external power source.

Magellan's GPS 2000, GPS 4000, and Trail-blazer XL are designed to guide campers, backpackers, hunters, anglers, and other outdoor enthusiasts through backwoods, deserts, forests, and other wilderness areas worldwide. Magellan introduced the world's first commercial hand-held GPS receiver in 1989.

The Magellan GPS 2000 ($199) offers the user at-a-glance updates on location, directions to a specific destination, speed, and distance to destination. Its plotter screen will draw a picture of the course set, route followed, location of nearby landmarks stored in memory, and progress to the destination.

The GPS 2000 offers four different screens: position, pointer, plotter, and navigation. The graphic pointer steers the user toward the destination, constantly updating the distance and time to go. The navigation screen provides directional arrows and speed, bearing and distance information, and cross track error. The position screen offers latitude/longitude and other location system information, plus altitude data. It provides easy comparison to map data.

At 6.6 by 2.3 by 1.3 inches (about the size of a candy bar, the company notes), and a weight of 10 ounces, the unit is backpack-handy. It runs for up to twenty-four hours on four AA alkaline batteries.

Magellan's GPS 4000 ($249) adds to the GPS 2000 with enhanced mapping, plotting and navigating features, and many other capabilities. It saves up to 200 landmarks and as many as five routes with twenty legs each. It updates progress in real time and shows the course as you move and all landmarks in your field of view. An adjustable scale plotter pans in any direction to view other portions of your route.

The user of the GPS 4000 can use a "go to" button to sketch the path to any landmark, or move the cursor to create one. For twenty-five of the landmarks you enter, you can also attach a two-line message about that location.

The Magellan Trailblazer XL ($299) offers the widest viewing screen of any compact GPS receiver, say company staff. Features include a real-time track plotter, six graphical navigation screens, sunrise/sunset calculation, multiple map datums and coordinate systems, and a variety of mapping functions.

The Trailblazer XL weighs in at 14 ounces and measures 6 by 3.5 by 1.3 inches Its large keys work even when operated by gloved hands, and it runs continuously for up to six hours on three AA alka-

(courtesy Johnson Worldwide Associates)

Silva Type 30 compass

line batteries.

Silva compasses are built with Swedish-steel needles mounted on a friction-free sapphire-jewel bearing. They perform accurately at temperatures between minus 40 degrees and 140 degrees Fahrenheit. Compass housings are ultrasonically welded and pressure filled with a clear anti-static liquid.

New in the Silva line is the Type 25 Ranger Pro, an upgrade of the classic Ranger 15CL compass, with a longer base plate, silicon map gripper, improved V site, larger base plate numbers, and other improvements. The Type 30 Omni is a keyring/zipper pull compass in a base-plate construction.

Also new is the Silva Type 40W Wristband compass, for taking bearings at a glance. It can be easily attached to a web, plastic, or leather watch band.

The popular Silva Polaris and Starter 1–2–3 starter compasses now have a contoured back on the baseplate and larger graduation lines and numbers.

Sources

American Camper
Nelson/Weather-Rite
P.O. Box 14488
Lenexa, KS 66285–4488
(913) 492–3200
Fax: (913) 492–8749

Brunton
620 East Monroe
Riverton, WY 82501
(307) 856–6559
Fax: (307) 856–1840

Eagle Electronics
P.O. Box 669
Catoosa, OK 74015–0669
(800) 932–4534

Garmin
1200 East 151st Street
Olathe, KS 66062
(913) 397–8200
Fax: (913) 397–8282

Lowrance Electronics
12000 East Skelly Drive
Tulsa, OK 74128–2486

Magellan Systems Corp.
960 Overland Court
San Dimas, CA 91773
(909) 394–5000
Fax: (909) 394–7050

Normark Corporation
10395 Yellow Circle Drive
Minnetonka, MN 55343
(612) 933–7060
Fax: (612) 933–0046

Silva
Johnson Worldwide Associates
Camping Division
1326 Willow Road
Sturtevant, WI 53177
(800) 848–3673
Fax: (414) 884–1703
E-mail: camping@racine.jwa.com

US Geological Survey Map Sales
Box 25286, Federal Center
Denver, CO 80225
(703) 648–4000

Chapter 16
Setting Your Sights While Camping

Car-campers and backpackers share the delights of sights. Landmarks and wildlife are lures that draw us outdoors, and optics—binoculars and telescopes—help us get a closer look. Here are some details on the equipment available, and how it can be used to increase camping fun.

Optic Option

A *telescope* is a device that uses glass lenses to magnify (make it appear larger and closer than it really is) the scene on which it is focused.

A *binocular*—note that each is a singular—is a pair of telescopes mounted so that the view of each eye is merged into one scene in the brain. Binoculars and telescopes share something else; a numerical code that tells us how they perform, once we crack the code. More campers probably use binoculars than telescopes, so the code will be explained for binoculars.

Basic Info

Three features are key to any magnifying optics:
- *Magnification* is how close it makes things appear;
- *Resolution* is how sharp the image looks in the lens; and
- *Light transmission* is the brightness of the view.

All three must be in balance and match the job you have for it.

Cracking the Code

You've probably seen a binocular's numerical designation; 7x35 is a common one. The first number, 7x, indicates the power or magnification. In this case, the image you see when you look through the binocular is seven times as large as when you look with only your eyes.

The second number is diameter in millimeters of the lens farthest from the eye. That's the objec-

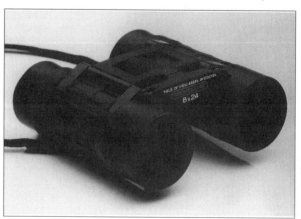

Redfield Water-Resistant Compact Binoculars

(courtesy Redfield)

tive lens, and its diameter determines how much light enters the binocular, most of it ultimately to carry the image to your eye. Higher magnification power requires a larger objective lens. A bigger lens adds brightness and resolution, which is better in low-light. If most of your viewing is to be in bright conditions, you might want a smaller objective lens.

The field of view is the scene you see, presented in the width in feet of the scene you see at 1,000 yards, or the angle of that view in degrees. Generally, the higher the magnifying power, the smaller the field of view. A standard 7x35 binocular takes in 340 feet of view at 1,000 yards; a 10x50 binocular sees about 272 feet at the same distance. To convert a field of view angle to feet, remember that each degree of view translates to about 52 feet at 1,000 yards.

Resolution is the binocular's ability to deliver fine detail to your eye. As a general rule, a larger objective lens delivers more detail. Sharpness also depends on optical quality, light transmission, atmospheric conditions, optical and mechanical alignment, and your vision.

One key to optical quality is the glass used, in binocular prisms as well as lenses. BaK–4 prism glass is best, manufacturers say, with BK7 prism glass used to make more economical binoculars.

Coatings

Light enters the binocular through the objective lenses, but not all of it gets to your eyes. Some is absorbed by the glass components; some reflected off them. The loss of gathered light to reflection can be reduced by coatings. These add both quality and cost to the binocular.

There are several levels to optical coatings:
- *Coated* means that some selected lens and prism surfaces have been coated to improve light transmission.
- *Fully coated* means that all air-to-glass surfaces have been coated.
- *Multi-coated* means that one or

more surfaces have been coated with multiple films.
- *Fully multi-coated* means that all air-to-glass surfaces have been coated with multiple films.

At each step up the scale to fully multi-coated, as described above, the light transmission and cost of the binocular increases. One manufacturer says light transmission can range from 50 percent with minimal coating to 95 percent with full multi-coating.

Other coating options include Rubicon and ultraviolet coatings.

In Rubicon (ruby) coating fourteen layers of multi-coating filter out red light and provide brilliant daytime viewing. This is especially helpful when viewing scenes including brightly illuminated water, snow, or sand.

An ultraviolet (UVC) coating removes glare from excess ultraviolet rays for a clearer, more vivid image especially in bright sunlight.

Prism Principles

In all binoculars the light enters through the objective lens and travels through prisms to the eyepieces. It can take different routes, though. Two systems are used in today's binoculars: the classic, also known as Porro, and roof prisms.

Classic (Porro) prisms: Each side uses two prisms, in a system invented in 1823 by Ignatio Porro. The prisms are placed at right angles. These binoculars are easy to spot: the distance between the eyepieces is usually narrower than between the objective lenses. Some compact binoculars, though, feature Porro lenses with objective lenses closer together than the eyepieces.

Prism Preference

Roof prisms: The prisms are located one over the other. Objective and eyepieces line up. The binocular is smaller so it's easier to stash in pocket or backpack.

Which is better? Like every other item of camping equipment, it depends on how you'll use it. Roof-prism binoculars are much smaller and lighter, and thus easier to carry along on backpack or hiking outings.

Porro prism binoculars offer more depth in focus. They're larger, and because of savings in manufacturing costs, usually provide the best binocular for the dollar.

Beyond prism format, binoculars offer other options.

More Decisions

Wide-angle binoculars increase the field of view without cutting power. Generally, any binocular offering a field of view of about 400 feet or more at 1,000 yards (about 7.6 degrees) is considered a wide-angle binocular.

In the case above, 7.6 degrees is the real angle of view. It would be multiplied by the magnification, or x-factor, to determine the apparent view. In an 8x binocular, for example, the apparent angle of view would be about 60 degrees.

Zoom binoculars offer two power numbers. The binoculars can be set at either or at any magnification between them.

Fixed-focus binoculars have no focus mechanism. The distance at which they're in focus varies from person to person. These binoculars are pre-set focused on infinity, and will present fairly well focused images at distances from about 40 feet at 7x, or 80 feet at 10x, to infinity. They're handy, but seldom deliver the sharpness of adjustable focus binoculars.

Long eye-relief binoculars are designed for people who wear eyeglasses, to avoid the "tunnel vision" they often get when looking through their glasses and binoculars at the same time. Folding back the rubber eyecups of regular binoculars trims this problem; long eye-relief binoculars do it even better.

Well Adjusted

Binoculars must be adjusted for a clear view. Most binoculars have a focus wheel or other mechanism that determines the distance at which the selected scene is in focus. Some waterproof models have separate focus mechanisms for each lens. Campers would seldom use these.

Diopter Adjuster

Focus only works when the two lenses have been adjusted to balance the vision variety between our eyes. The *diopter control*, a dial on the right lens, must be adjusted to match the vision of the user. Most of us have one eye stronger than the other, and it's necessary to balance this with the binocular to avoid headaches and eyestrain. Here's how to do this:

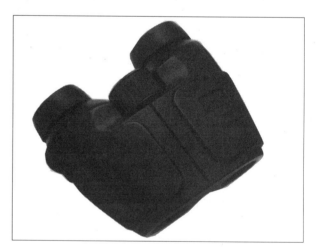

Bausch & Lomb Legacy 8x24

- look through the binocular and spread the tubes the distance apart that renders one clear circular image;
- set the right diopter at 0, then cover the right front lens and turn the focus knob until your left eye clearly sees a subject that is at least 20 feet away;

Bausch & Lomb Legacy 10x25

Brunton InteliOptics rangefinding binocular

- without moving, cover the left front lens, and turn the right lens diopter until the scene is again clear; and
- note the setting on the diopter, so you can return to it each time you use the binocular.

Products/Services

Bausch & Lomb's top-of-the-line Elite 8x ($1,455) and 10x ($1,520) roof prism binoculars are now available in waterproof/fogproof configurations. Both feature PC–3 phase correction coating, multi-coating on all air-to-glass surfaces, and silver coating on prism-reflecting surfaces. They offer long eye relief with roll-down rubber eyecups.

Bausch & Lomb's Legacy Compact ($254) 8x 24 is now waterproof, too. It is just 4 inches high, to fit in a jacket pocket. It features multi-coated optics and BaK–4 prisms. The Legacy series also includes two folding roof-prism models, the 8x22 ($85) and 10x25 ($87), both with multi-coated optical elements and fold-down eyecups providing long eye relief for eyeglass wearers.

Bnox FunSeeker binoculars ($12) prove that not all optical products are pricey. FunSeekers are waterproof, with acrylic lenses that offer 99-percent UV protection. They weigh just 4 ounces, and measure 2 by 2 by 4 inches. Magnification is pre-focused, with models available at 5.2x and 7x powers.

Brunton's line of fine optics includes the new Eterna waterproof binoculars ($407–$430), which are filled with nitrogen so they won't fog internally. Long eye relief and PopDown eyecups offer a full field of view, even to the eyeglass wearer. Starfire multi-coated optics block out 96.9 percent of ultraviolet and infrared light and eliminate glare. By combining BaK–4 prisms and advanced multi-coatings, company personnel say, Eterna binoculars offer clear views on dark and sunny days. They're available in 7x42, 10x50, and 8x40 models.

New Eterna waterproof compact binoculars ($337–$349) offer the same features in compact 8x 24 and 10x25 configurations.

Brunton's Lite Tech compact series binoculars ($102) are described by company staff as the first completely waterproof optics at an affordable price. They feature BaK–4 prisms and fully coated optics for maximum light transmission and clarity, and come in 8x25 and 10x25 models.

Brunton recently introduced its InteliOptics electronic rangefinder binocular ($793–$833), which it calls a "marriage between sophisticated electronics and display techniques with advanced optics design." It features an LCD in the optical path to display range-finding data. Large buttons on the right side of the binocular control rangefinding, which is computed by a microprocessor by comparing an animal seen at a distance to a prestored average animal height.

(courtesy The Brunton Company)

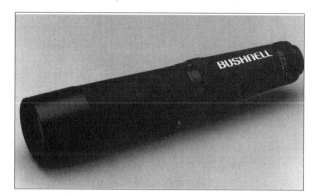

Bushnell Natureview 15-45x60 Spotting Scope

Nikon 10x42 Attaché

(courtesy Nikon Sport Optics)

Bushnell Banner Sentry Waterproof Spotting Scope

Nikon 7x50 IF Sports & Marine binocular

(courtesy Nikon Sport Optics)

Bushnell has its eye on anglers, with its new 8x 25 Angler ($117) binocular, which has a built-in Polarizing filter to cut surface glare for a clear look into the water. The compact, 3.5-inch Porro-prism binocular fits into a fishing vest. Its optics are fully coated.

The Bushnell Powerview Series now includes a 12x50 model ($81), which provides high magnification with high light gathering ability. It can be used with a tripod.

The Bushnell Natureview series was designed specifically for naturalists and bird watchers. Its new 8x30 ($138) compact focuses as closely as 8 feet, with extended eye relief for eyeglass wearers. All air-to-glass surfaces are magnesium fluoride coated.

Bushnell now offers its waterproof/fogproof 18–36x50 Banner Sentry spotting scope ($233). It

offers wide field viewing at low power and sharp close-up detail at high power. Its coated prismatic lenses boost light transmission. The 15–45x60 Natureview Spotting Scope ($239) converts to a zoom telephoto lens (for example 15x equals f/9 at 560 mm: 54 equals f/28 at 1,680 mm) for most single lens reflex cameras with the addition of the camera mount provided with the scope and a camera body adapter.

Nikon has a full line of top-quality binoculars, including its new Attaché 8x42 ($370) and 10x42 ($498) full size binoculars. Longer eye relief gives eyeglass wearers a field of view as full as that seen by a person without glasses. They also feature a close focus distance of just 16 feet, making them especially useful for birders and wildlife watchers.

New all-weather 7x50 IF Sports & Marine individual focus binoculars from Nikon specialize in low-light conditions. A standard 7x 50 IF Sports & Marine ($368) is available, as is a similar

Nikon Waterproof 16-47x60 SpotterxL Outfit

(courtesy Nikon Sport Optics)

Olympus Stylish Vision Ultracompact binocular

model, the 7x50 IF Compass ($500) with built-in compass and distance scale. They're waterproof, fogproof, and shock-resistant with easy-to-grip rubber armor. With the individual focus system, each lens focuses to meet the requirements of the user's eye, so no additional focusing is required.

Veteran birders, serious wildlife observers, and professional binocular users can now look at and through the Nikon 10x42 Superior E Porro prism binocular ($1,205) with the latest in optical design and engineering technology.

Nikon's Spring binocular series combines a compact size with optical features that deliver quality viewing. Available in two central focus models—8x21 ($124) and 10x21 ($140)—they offer 10-foot minimum-focus distance, wide field of

Olympus Pathfinder binocular

view, and handy and lightweight design.

Earth & Sky binoculars from Nikon are designed for avid birders and wildlife observers. They offer true long eye relief for eyeglass wearers. They include the Lemur 7x35 ($216), Talon 8x40 ($238), Kestrel 10x50 ($265), and Wolverine 7x50 ($261).

Nikon's new 16–47x60 SpotterxL spotting scope ($700) is designed to be slim, tough, and light. It's guaranteed fogproof and waterproof. All lenses are fully multi-coated, with a special phase correction coating applied to the roof prism glass to prevent light loss or reduced resolving power. It weighs 26½ ounces and is 12½ inches long. It is also available as the SpotterxL Outfit ($800), with a compact Slik field tripod and carrying case.

Olympus' new Trooper binocular line offers three models: 10x50 DPS ($110), 8x40 DPS ($90), and 7x35 DPS ($80).

Troopers, described as affordable and rugged for a wide range of outdoor viewing, feature coated lenses for high-image brightness, contrast, and quality. All three models have a central focus knob and diopter corrector. Each includes a carrying case and strap. They range in weight from 22.9 ounces (7x35 DPS) to 28.6 ounces (10x50 DPS).

The new Olympus Sahara compact Porro prism binocular is lightweight, easy to carry, and affordable. Each of the three models—12x24 PCII ($160), 10x24 PCII ($150), and 8x24 PCII ($140)—features coated lenses and a focusing dial. They also

Pentax 8x21 and 10x21 UCF Mini binocular

have prisms made of BaK–4 glass, foldable rubber eyecups, and weigh 8.8 ounces each.

The Olympus Outback binocular, available in the 10x25 RCII ($160) or 8x22 RCII ($150) models, is weatherproof, with all-weather seals to keep out moisture and dust.

For a good look at nature, Olympus offers the new Pathfinder, with four models ranging from the 12x50 EXPS ($260) to the 7x50 EXPS ($240). They feature multi-coated lenses, and non-slip, rubber-clad bodies.

Olympus Stylus Vision Ultracompact binoculars are slim and flat, with 8x15 RF ($320) and 6x12 RF ($280) models. They weigh only 5.1 ounces each.

Pentax binoculars are made with high-refraction BaK–4 glass prisms to gather more light and reduce vignetting. Important optical elements are multi-coated, and Pentax binoculars are encased in rubber housings to protect them from shock and damage, and make holding them more comfortable.

Long eye relief is available in most Pentax binoculars so the entire field of view is visible, even when wearing eyeglasses.

Pentax UCF Series offers four types of Porro-prism binoculars: all purpose, weather-resistant, zoom, and pocket-size. A dual-axis system prevents misalignment of lens barrels, which Pentax experts say is a major cause of eye fatigue.

Pentax PCF III Series binoculars feature a center-focusing system with a focus lock, a click-stop diopter adjuster, fold-back eyepieces, and a tripod

socket for extended use.

For serious binocular users Pentax offers its DCF Series, slender, lightweight, straight-line design binoculars with large-aperture multi-coated lenses, click-stop diopter adjuster, tripod socket, and other features.

The Pentax PIF Series is made for rough duty, with waterproof construction rated to 16.5 feet down, full-body rubber housing, and nitrogen-filled body to prevent fogging from sudden temperature changes.

The Pentax 7x20 and 8x30 monoculars are

(courtesy Tasco)

Tasco Compact Binocular

very versatile, because they provide both telescopic and microscopic abilities. The 7x20 offers 22x microscopic magnification; the 8x30 provides 25x power. The smaller 7x20 measures just 3.8 inches

(courtesy Redfield)

Redfield Waterproof Camo Binocular with Compass

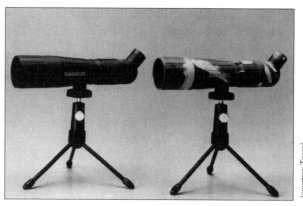

(courtesy Tasco)

Tasco Mini Spotting Scopes

long and weighs 2.1 ounces.

Redfield's All Sports Widefield Binoculars feature roof prism design, and coated precision-ground lenses. Waterproof Armor Coat Binoculars are available in 7x35 and 10x50 models, both with vinyl case. Waterproof Camo Binoculars with Compass are available in the same configurations, with a compass housed in the adjustment dial. Water-Resistant Compact Binoculars, less than 4 inches long, offer wide-angle views in 8x24.

Redfield spotting scopes include the Regal IV, which the company calls its premier scope for spotting, target shooting, and bird watching. The water-resistant scope has black rubber armor coating, separate front focus, and straight-through viewing. It comes with 25x and 20x–60x zoom eyepieces. The Waterproof Spotting Scope is a lightweight, 20x–45x scope that comes with a vinyl carrying case and flip-up objective lens cover.

Redfield spotting scopes can be fitted with adapter tubes and T-mounts for use as camera lenses.

Tasco's newest compact binocular is a 6x16 mm model ($199) that fits in the palm of your hand. It only weighs about 5 ounces.

Tasco binoculars also include the Futura-LE line, with extended eye relief for eyeglass wearers. New models include a 12x25 mm compact ($186), and 10x–30x50 zoom ($390). The line features center focus, fully coated optics and Rubicon-coated objective lenses.

Tasco Sonoma rubber armored binoculars feature ruby-coated objective lenses, fully coated optics, and soft-rubber armor. The line includes compact and full-size models.

Tasco has also added wide-angle models in its compact binocular line ($93), plus new zoom binocular models ($534 and $713).

Tasco is offering two new mini-spotting scopes ($113). They differ only in their rubber armor: one in black and one in camouflage. Both feature a 20x scope with 40 mm objective lens. They're each 8.5 inches long and weigh just over 11 ounces, with ball-and-socket tripods, rubber-tipped feet, and a soft padded pouch.

Sources

Bausch & Lomb
Bushnell Corp.
9200 Cody Street
Overland Park, KS 66214
(800) 423–3537
Web site: www.bushnell.com

Bnox, Inc.
(800) 869–2669

Brunton
620 East Monroe
Riverton, WY 82501
(307) 856–6559
Fax: (307) 856–1840

Bushnell Corp.
9200 Cody Street
Overland Park, KS 66214
(800) 423–3537
Web site: www.bushnell.com

Nikon Sport Optics
1300 Walt Whitman Road
Melville, NY 11747–3064
(800) 645–6687

Olympus America, Inc.
Two Corporate Center Drive
Melville, NY 11747–3157
(516) 844–5000
Web site: www.olympusamerica.com

Pentax Corporation
35 Inverness Drive East
Englewood, CO 80112
(303) 799–8000

Redfield
5800 East Jewell Ave.
Denver, CO 80224
(303) 757–6411
Fax: (303) 756–2338

Tasco Customer Service Department
P.O. Box 520080
Miami, FL 33152–0080
(305) 591–3670, ext. 288

Bibliography

Chapter 1 Let's Camp!

Griffin, Steven A. "Happy Campers," *Outdoor Action*, Aug. 1995, page 85 (reprinted by permission).

Chapter 2 Camping Comfort Is in the Bag

Johnston, Greg (*Seattle Post-Intelligencer*). "Tents and Sleeping Bags Can Make or Break a Trip," *Midland Daily News*, May 28, 1996.

Judd, Ron C. Wrap Session, *Seattle Times*, Feb. 15, 1996.

Sharp, Eric. The Right Sleeping Bag Guarantees Good Camping, *Detroit Free Press*, April 30, 1996.

Chapter 3 Tents: Gimme Shelter

Griffin, Steve. Spending Night in Tent can be Real Experience, *Midland Daily News*, July 21, 1988.

Johnston, Greg (*Seattle Post-Intelligencer*). "Tents and Sleeping Bags Can Make or Break a Trip," *Midland Daily News*, May 28, 1996.
Griffin, Steve. "Good Campers Can't Camp Without Lots of Gadgets," *Midland Daily News*, June 2, 1991

Chapter 4 Backpacking

Kerasote, Ted. "No Matter How Clear the Water, Purify it Before Taking a Drink," *Sports Afield*, May 1993, 28.

Chapter 5 Family Camping

Griffin, Steve. "Blueberry Bounty," *Country America*, June 1990 (adapted).

Chapter 6 Camp Clothing

Staffs of *The Footwear News,* and *SportStyle,* "The Basics: The Right Boot," date unknown.
—"The Basics: Lugging It Out," date unknown.
—"The Basics: Drying It Out," date unknown.

Chapter 9 Camp Cooking

Gunn, Carolyn, and the editors of *Backpacker Trail Foods: Easy, Healthy and Delicious,* Emmaus, Pa.: Rodale Press, 1993.

Chapter 10 What's Bugging You?: Insects, Sun, and Poisonous Plants

Blumenthal, Deborah. "A New Breed of Light Clothing Blocks the Sun's Harmful Rays," *The New York Times,* May 22, 1996.

Consumer Reports. "Bug Off! How to Repel Biting Insects," *Consumer Reports,* July 1993, 451.

Hair, Marty. Review of *Nature's Revenge: The Secrets of Poison Ivy, Poison Oak, Poison Sumac and their Remedies* by Susan Carol Hauser. *Detroit Free Press,* April 9, 1996.

Hamilton, William P. "Getting Under Your Skin," *Backpacker,* April 1996, 30.

Holmes, Hannah. "The Battle of the Bugs," *Backpacker*, April 1996, 68.

Lalley, Heather. "Scratch Mosquitoes from Summer," *Detroit Free Press,* July 9, 1996.

New York Department of Public Health. "Background Information on DEET," NYDPH Bureau of Toxic Substance Assessment; 1991.

Orlow, Dr. Seth (Associated Press). "Children Need Extra Protection from the Sun," *Detroit Free Press,* May 21, 1996.

Sawyer Products. *Sawyer Solutions: A Practical Guide to Outdoor Protection.* Sawyer Products, Safety Harbor, Fla., 1994.

Chapter 11 Good Housekeeping

Griffin, Steve. "Beaverton's Gilson Tries to Make Your Park Visit Better," *Midland Daily News,* Aug. 17, 1995.

VanDerWerge, David. "Low-impact Camping: Loving Nature Softly," *Outdoor Ethics,* Summer 1989.

Chapter 12 Camping at the Extremes

Griffin, Steve. "Deer Camp Hunting in Michigan," *Michigan Living,* Nov. 1983 (adapted).

Hodgson, Michael. *America's Secret Recreation Areas,* San Francisco: Foghorn Press, 1993.

Kerasote, Ted. "Camping in Snow with Comfort," *Sports Afield,* Jan. 1993, 24.

Chapter 13 Canoe Camping

Sharp, Eric. "For the Best Canoe Trip Spend a Night on the River," *Detroit Free Press,* May 18, 1996.

Chapter 16 Getting Your Bearings

Gibbs, Jerry. "Satellite Navigation for Civilian Budgets," *Outside,* April 1996, 134.

Chapter 17 Setting Your Sights While Camping

Nikon's Guide to Observing Birds and Other Wildlife, Nikon and National Wildlife Federation, Melville, N.Y.

Index